Dedication
&
Acknowledgments

This book is dedicated to all of my students. Their questions and thirst for more crazy designs keep me writing. Thanks Ladies!

My deepest thanks to Slayton Shaw for his selfless willingness to answer my questions about Adobe InDesign and Illustrator software applications.

Appreciation to all of the other crazy quilters who post on Crazy Quilt International, Crazy Quilt Divas and other message boards about their love of crazy quilting. You have become a wonderful community support group!

Thanks to Pam Kellogg and Katie Bock for working so tiredlessly on magazines that feature local crazy quilt artists and for letting me play along with you. Special thanks also to Katie Bock for taking over the Crazy Quilt Journal Project so I could have the time to devote to drawing the seams in this book.

As always, many HUGS go to the ladies that sign up for my free online crazy quilt classes. You keep me motivated to create. Thank you from the bottom of my heart!

Table of Contents

Introduction

Quilts that are traditionally pieced will most often have no embellishments added. The exceptions are Art Quilts and Crazy Quilts. Art Quilts are viewed as a quilted canvas and can contain any type of embellishment. They may be pieced or worked on a solid foundation fabric. Traditionally, crazy quilts are pieced, usually in some seemingly random fashion, then embellished. While thread embroidery is a main element; modern crazy quilt embellishments can also include a wide range of ribbon embroidery, lace, trims, buttons, beads, sequins, and so forth.

Every seam of a Crazy Quilt can be embellished or just a select number of them can be embellished. The best way to determine this is to decide on the "style" of the quilt first before beginning to embroider.

Seams on a truly traditional style quilt can be "un-adorned" relying only on thread embroidery if the quilt is to be laundered. This type of style would showcase the maker's hand (or machine) embroidery talents.

Fancier crazy quilt creations are usually not laundered. These styles often include silk ribbon embroidery, beading, buttons, and other items along the seams.

Today, modern Crazy Quilts include a huge range of embellishing items that would not have been available to our Victorian quilters. If the 1800's seamstress had metallic fibers, silk cording, sequins, and beads available to her...I'm sure she would have included them in her fancy crazy quilt. Today, their is an endless list of possible embellishments when we consider the different possibilities for fibers, size/shape/color of beads and sequins, lace trims, ribbon trims, and such.

The 500 seam designs in this book include thread embroidery, silk ribbon embroidery, beads, sequins and buttons. You can consider including other elements or even changing the proposed elements.

Each seam design can be created in a range of colors; so, just because a seam is shown in blues for instance...that does not mean you can't create it in pinks. The colors in the designs do show relationships of same items within a specific seam.

Every seam begins with a basic embroidery stitch or a line of embroidery worked along a shape. These basic seams are shown in BLACK with the design, and are considered the Base Seam.

Other embroidery stitches (thread and/or ribbon) are worked on top of this base seam. More layers of embellishments can be added by sewing beads, sequins, or buttons to the seam. Sometimes, a button may be embellished or a fancy stitch used to attach it.

After you select your available threads, ribbons, beads, etc. then you can begin your stitching. Select a seam design and stitch the Base Seam first. This bas seam can be marked on your fabric by using the templates in the back of the book or can be free-hand stitched as well. Then layer other embroidery (thread and silk ribbon) and beads/buttons, etc. according to the selected seam design you have chosen.

You do not have to be a skilled master of the art of embroidery to create beautiful seams. If you have issues keeping your base seam uniformly spaced and the work neat; you might want to consider templating your base seam. It is also possible to template some of the additional embroidery stitches layered on top of the base seam.

At the back of the book, a set of templates is available for reproduction. These save countless hours once they are ready to use. It does take some time to create them however. The STITCH templates have "dots" marking the needle up/down positions of a specific embroidery stitch. So, these holes need to be "punched" so that a marking tool (like a pencil) can be inserted there to mark the fabric. The SHAPE templates need to be cut to the specific shape. These are then "traced around" to provide a line for stitching upon.

Common and simple stitches such as the Running Stitch, Outline Stitch, Stem Stitch, Blanket Stitch, and Chain Stitch can be created along the drawn line of a Shape Template. More complex stitches can sometimes be used as well, if they can be created to "follow a line".

If you do not want to create templates, that's perfectly fine as well. The seam designs will give you plenty of inspiration to create beautiful seams "free hand" without using any templates.

The book is organized into colored sections. At present, you are in the "general information" section. Next, the seam design are divided into two specific types: STITCH Template Seam Designs and SHAPE Template Seam Designs.

The Stitch Template Seam Designs includes seams that use the Chevron Stitch, Creten Stitch, Feather Stitch, Herringbone Stitch, or Straight Stitch as the embroidered Base Seam.

The Shape Template Seam Designs include familiar shapes such as Box, Circular, Curved, Polygons, and Others. Both types of designs include the Base Seam shown in BLACK. Other embroidery (thread or silk ribbon) and other embellishments in the individual seam designs are layered on top of the Base Seam.

If you are creating a traditional crazy quilt; you may want to omit the silk ribbon, beads, sequins, etc. and only create the thread embroidery Base Stitch embroidery. But, if you truly want a fully embellished quilt, then add all of the elements sown in the seam design. You can also chose to add even more than is shown...get creative! More embroidery, ribbon flowers, beads, sequins, etc. added to this original seam design will just give the project more of your individual taste. So, don't be afraid to use different colors or different embellishing elements in these seam designs to make them appear even more complex.

Stitch Template Seam Designs

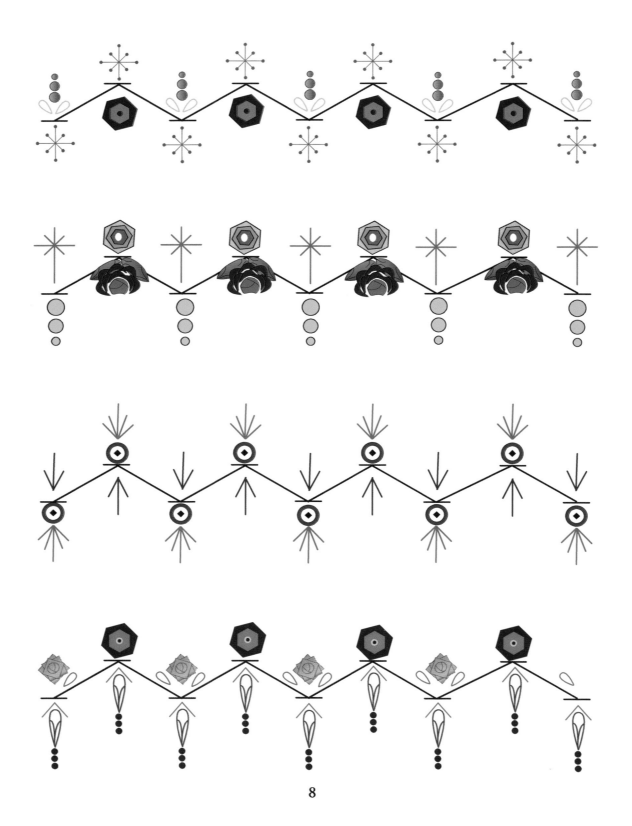

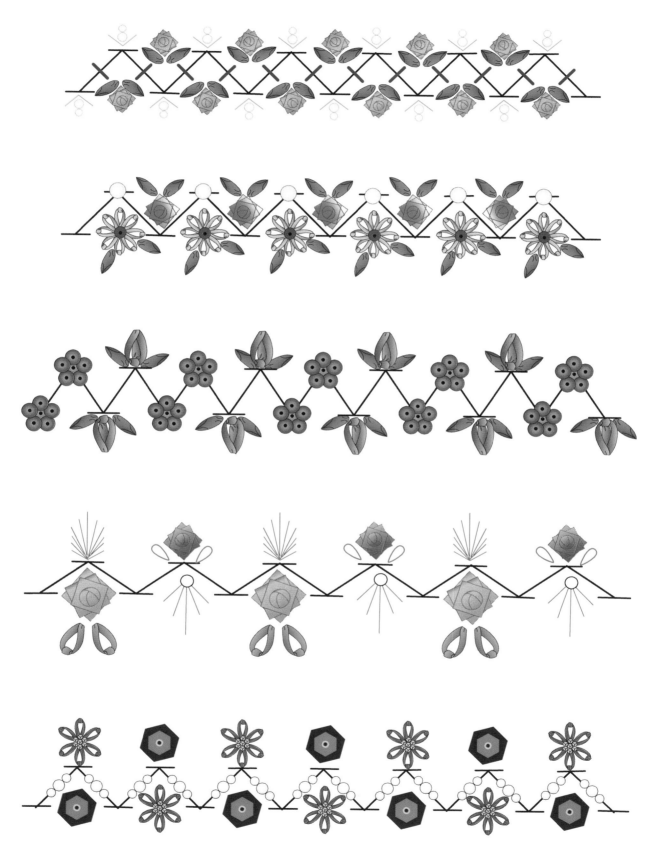

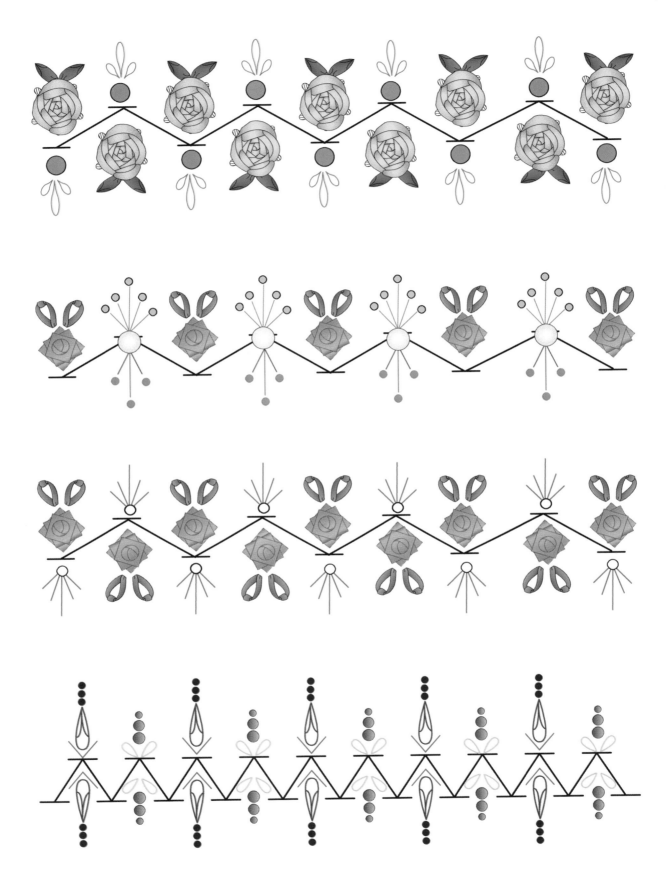

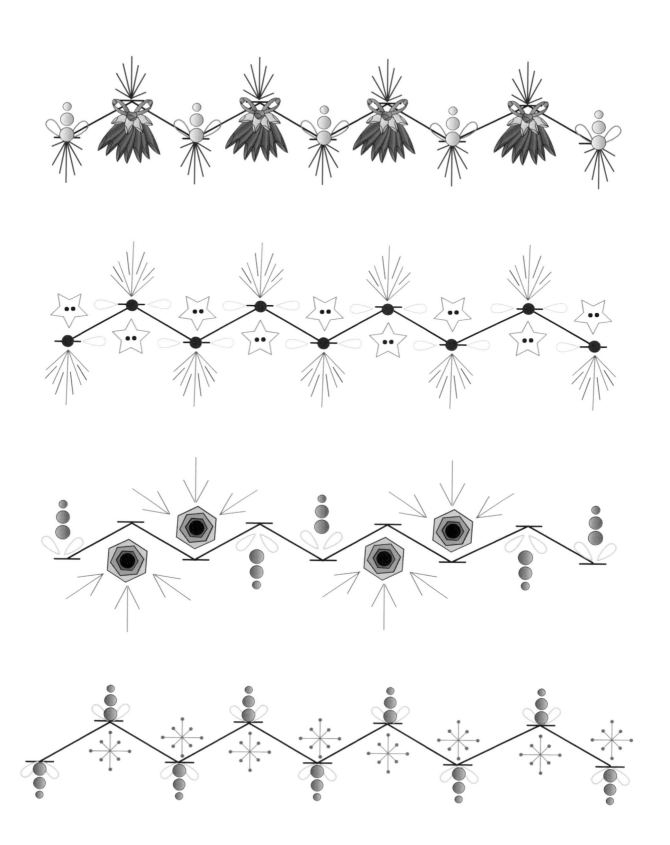

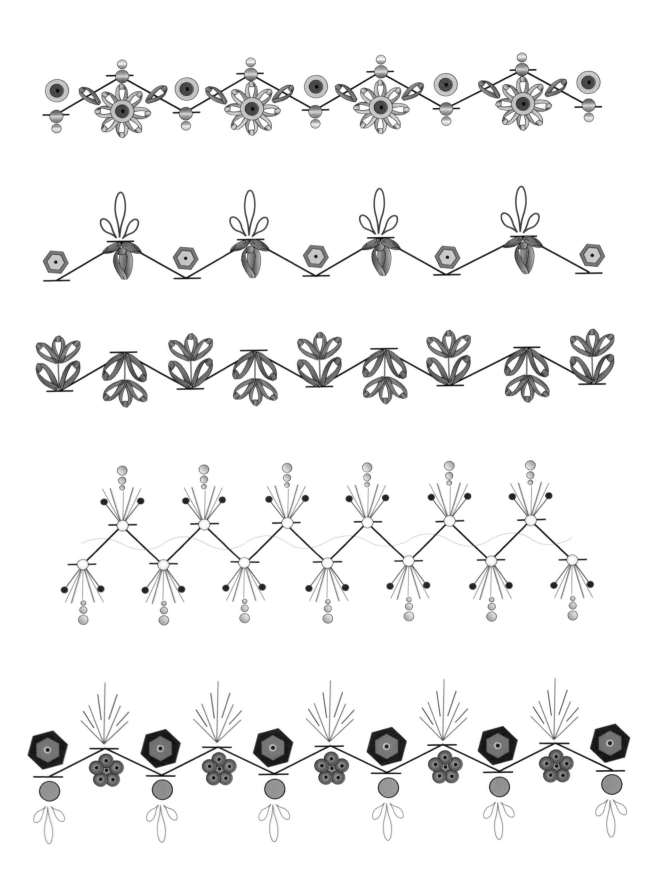

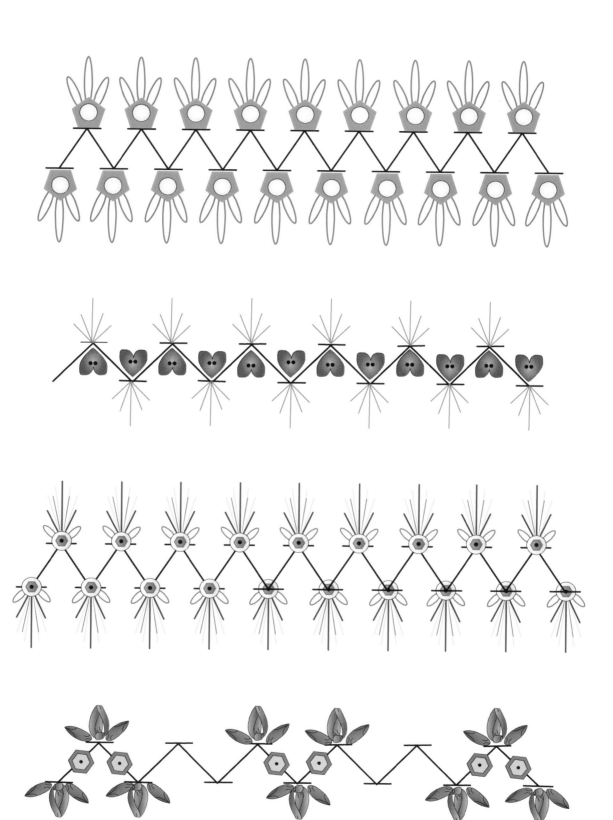

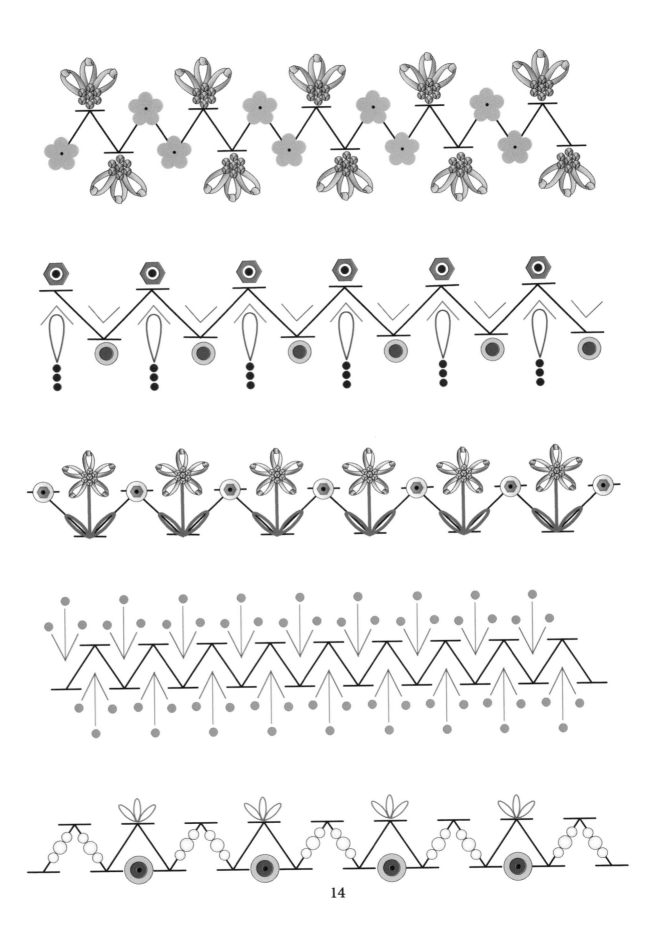

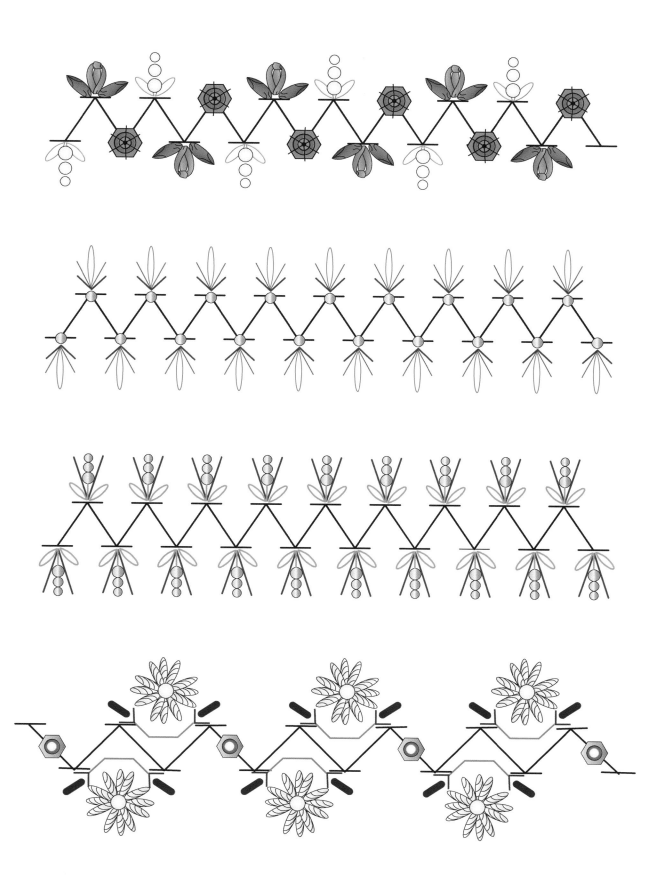

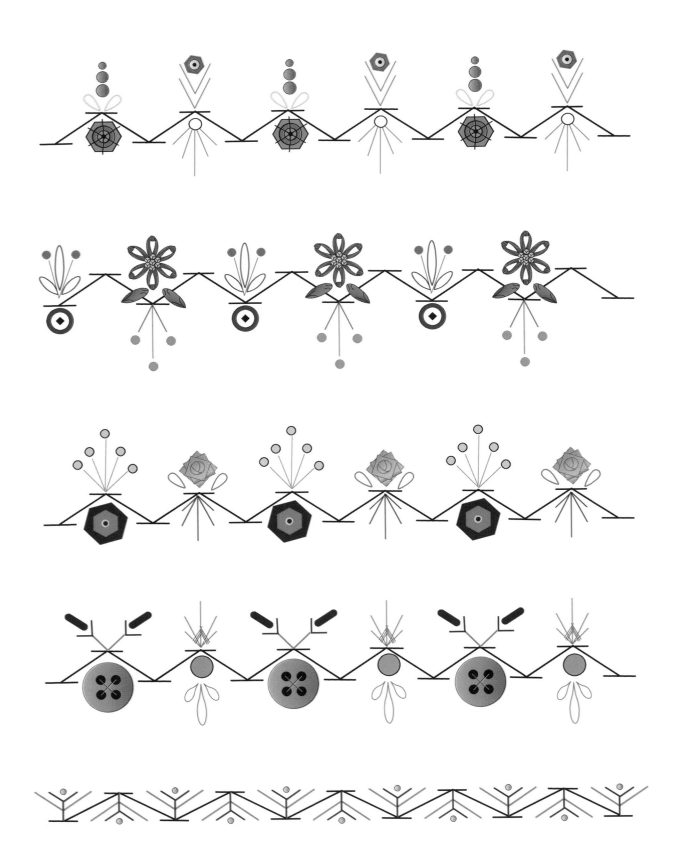

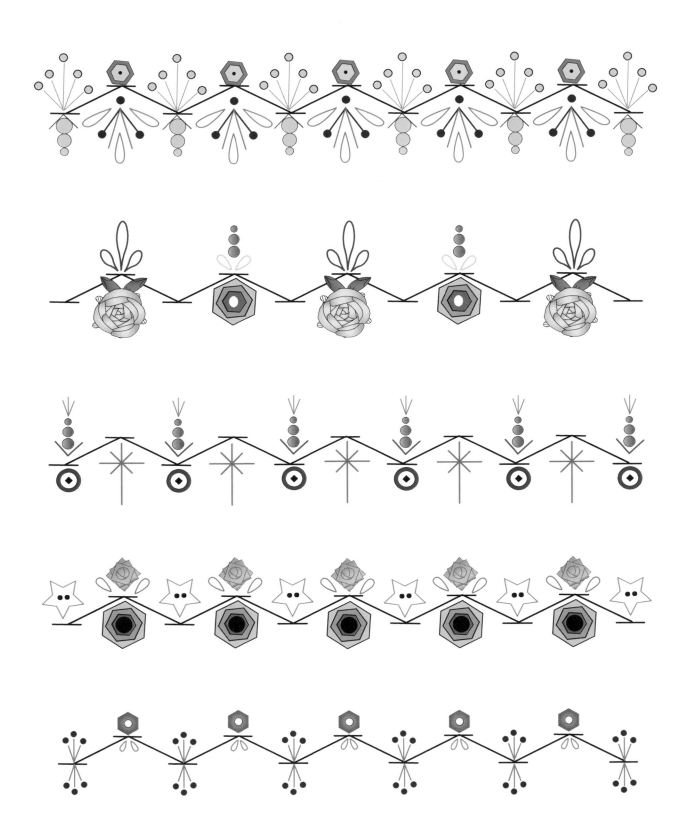

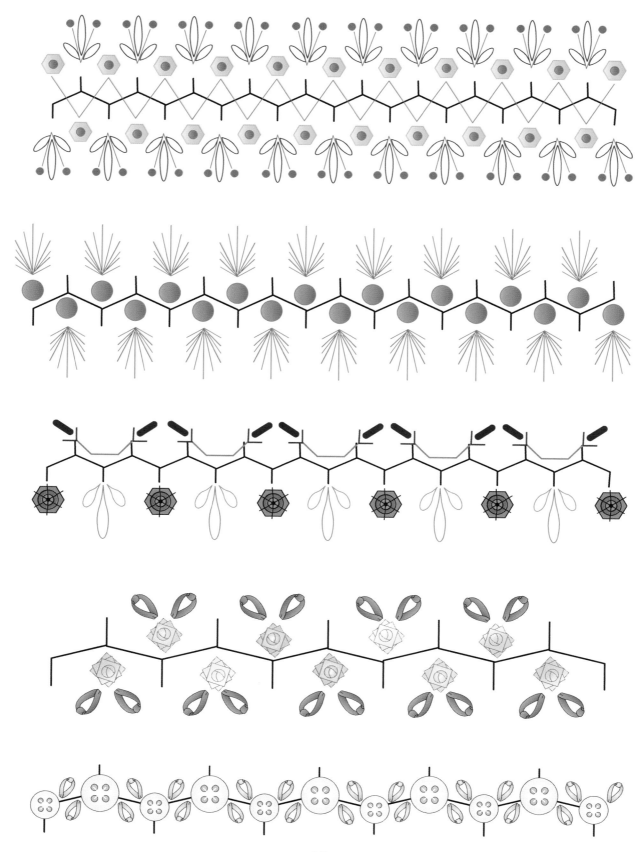

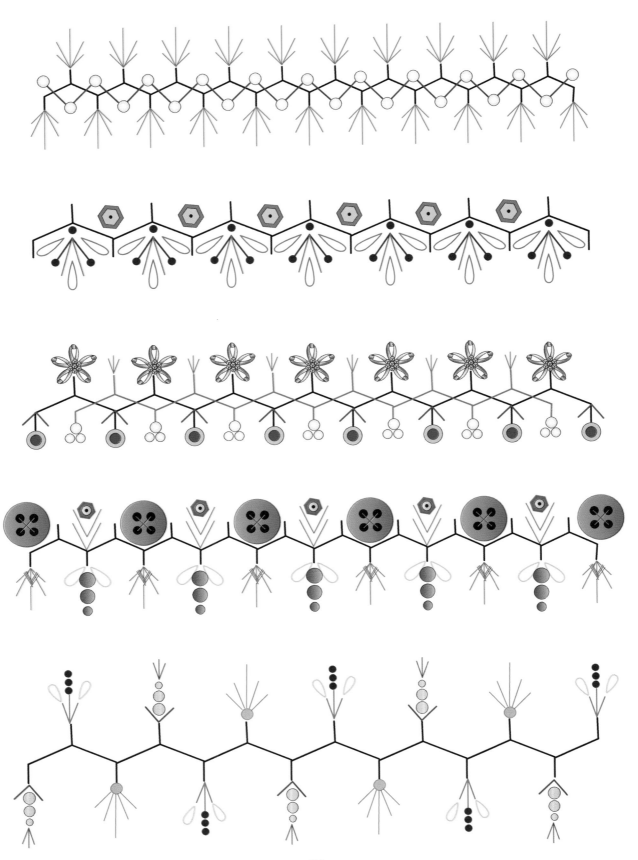

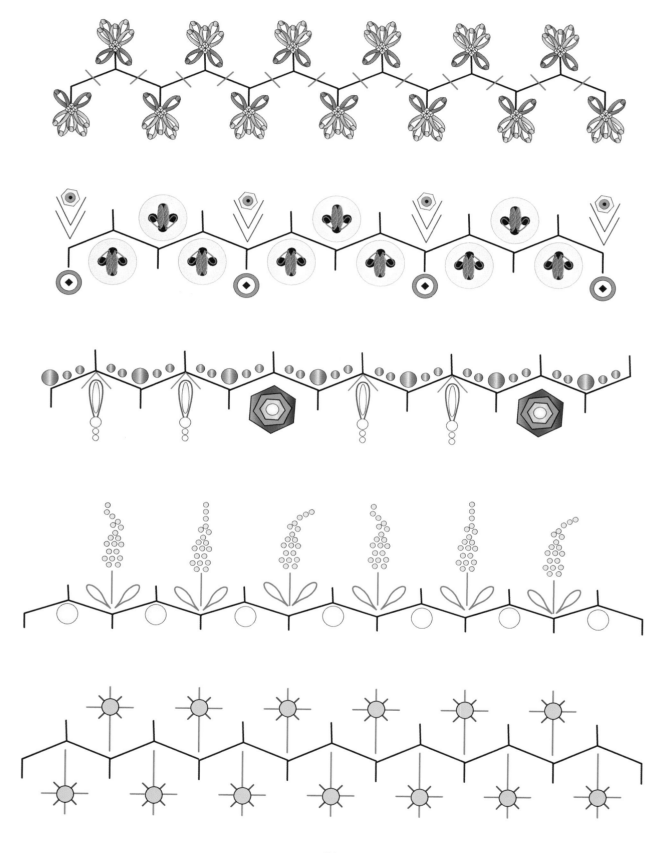

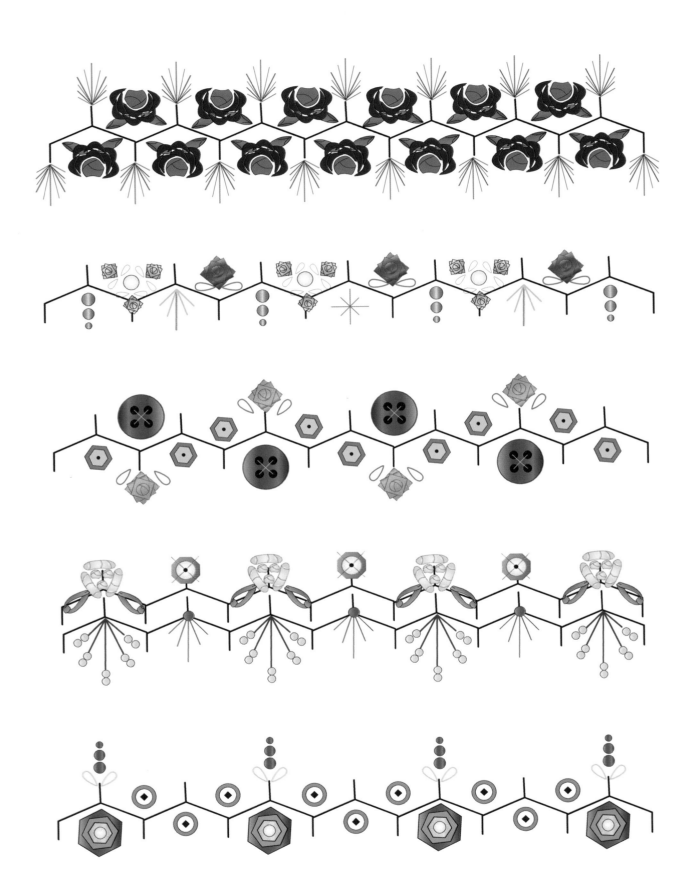

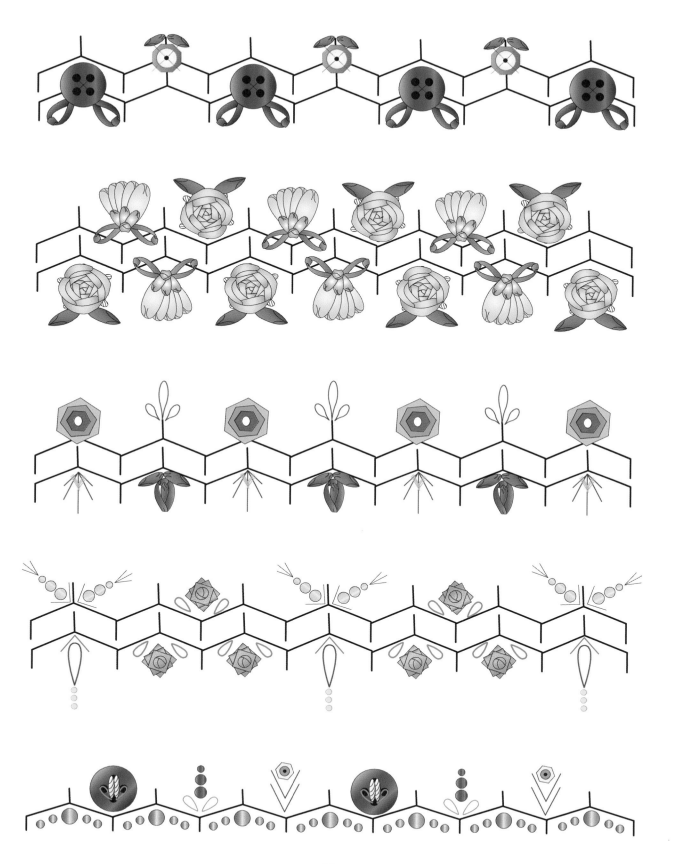

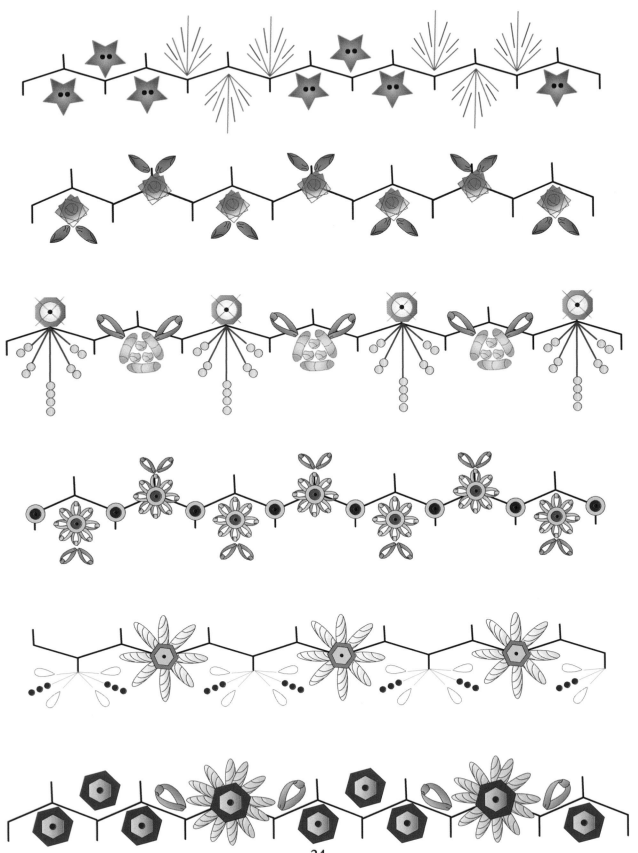

24

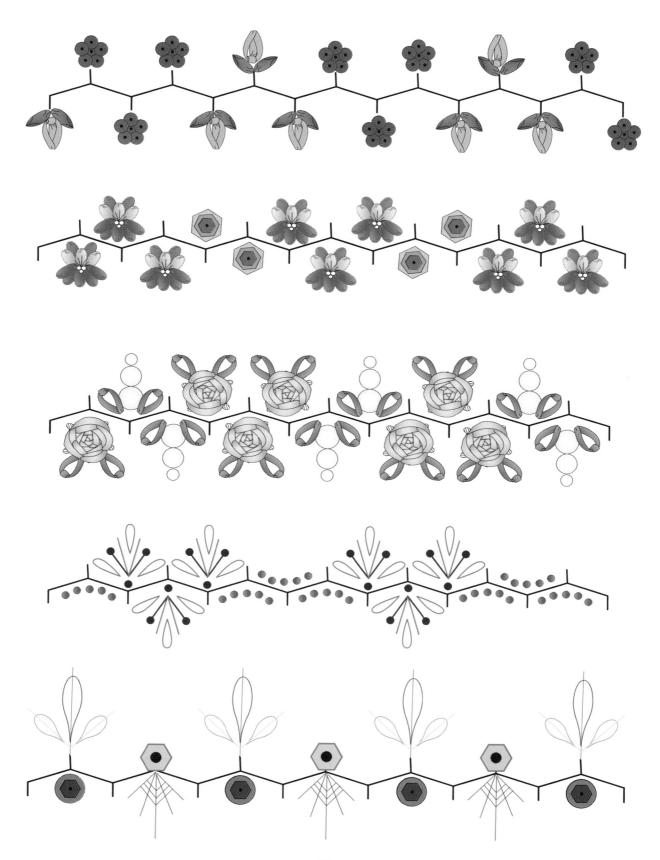

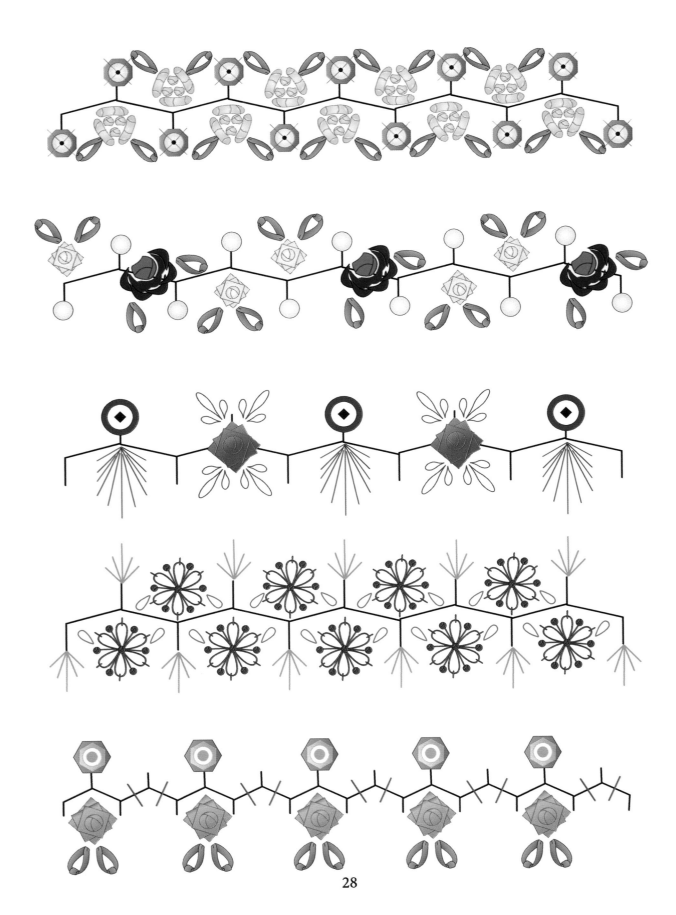

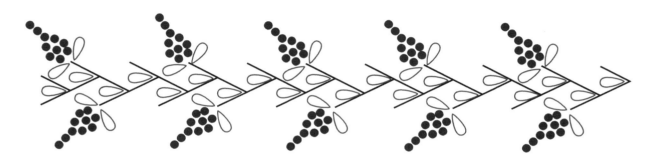

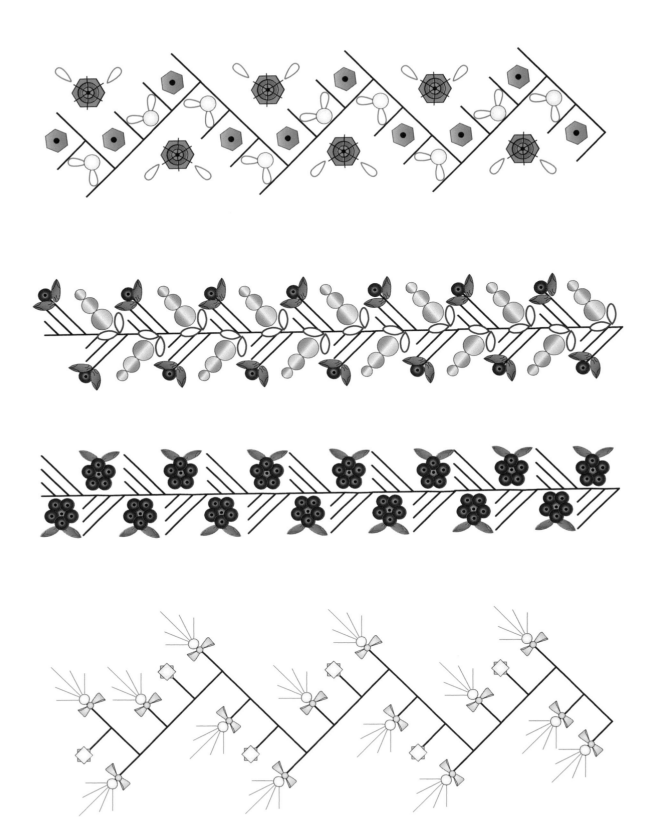

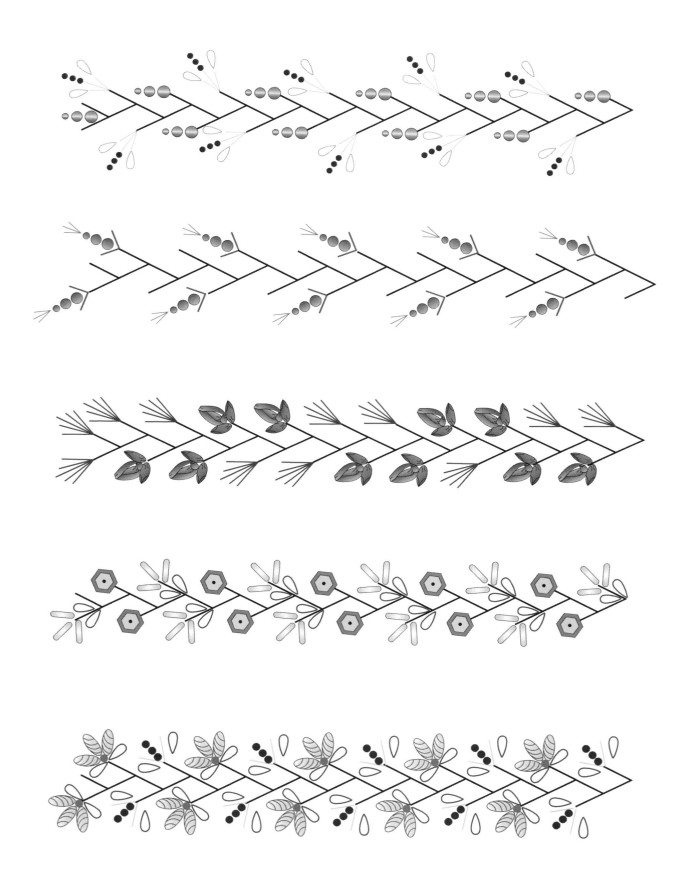

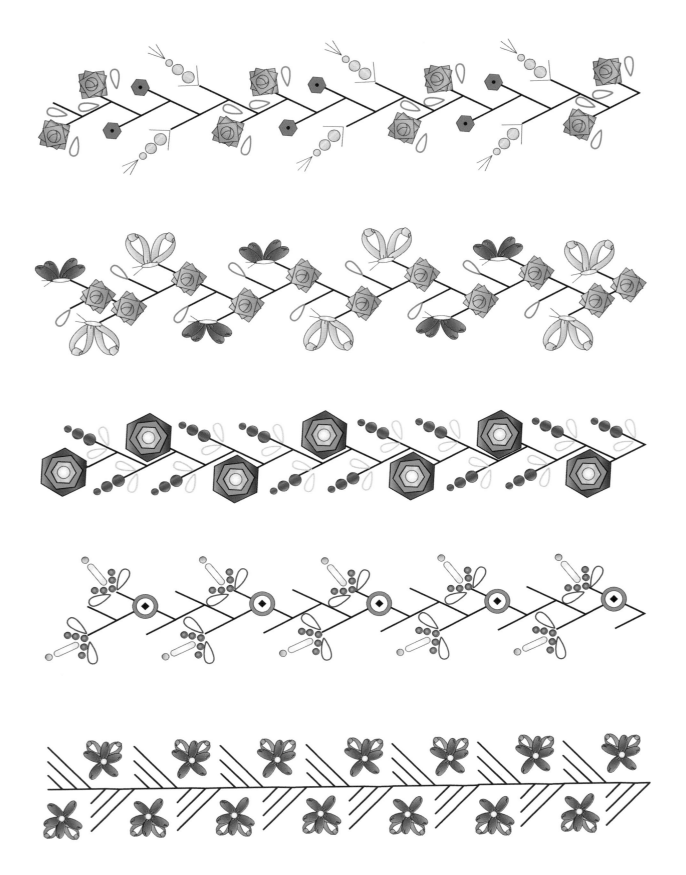

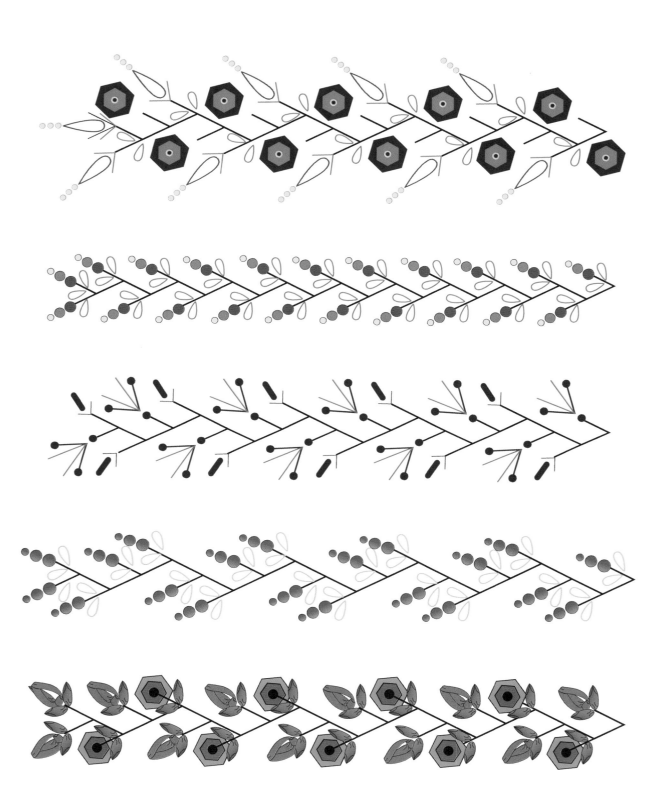

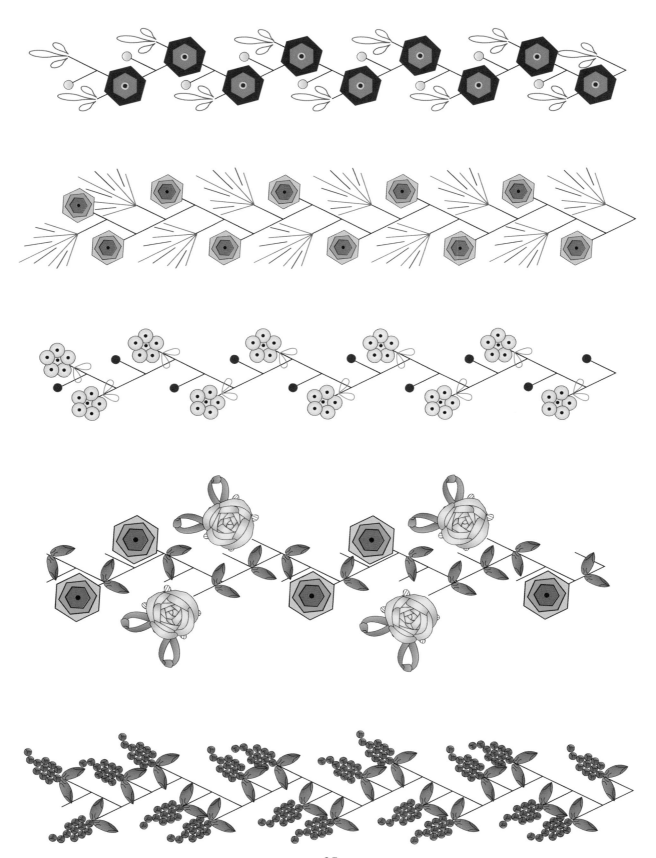

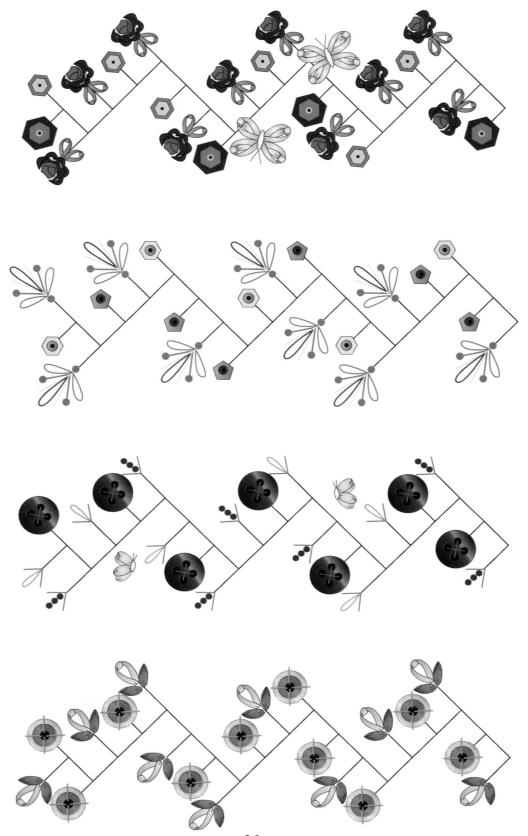

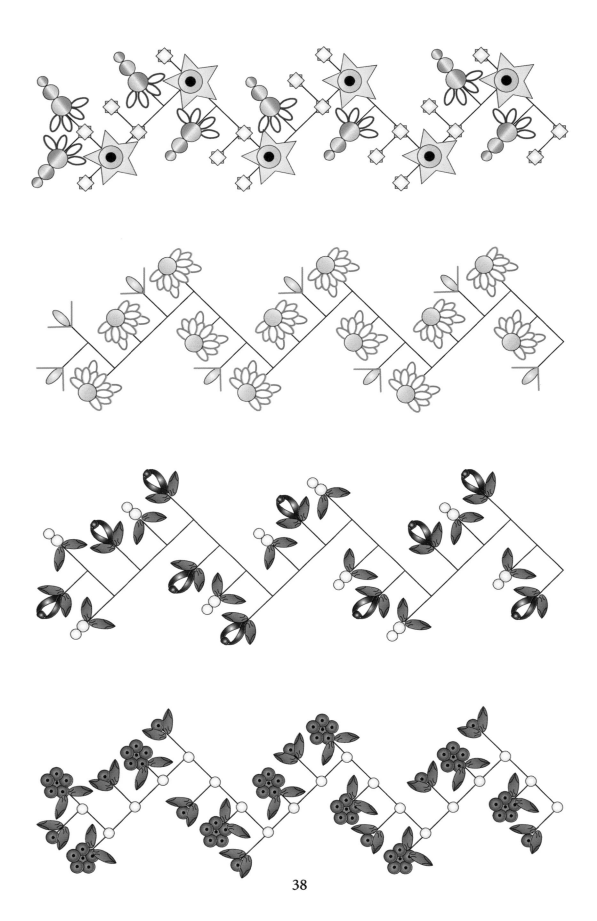

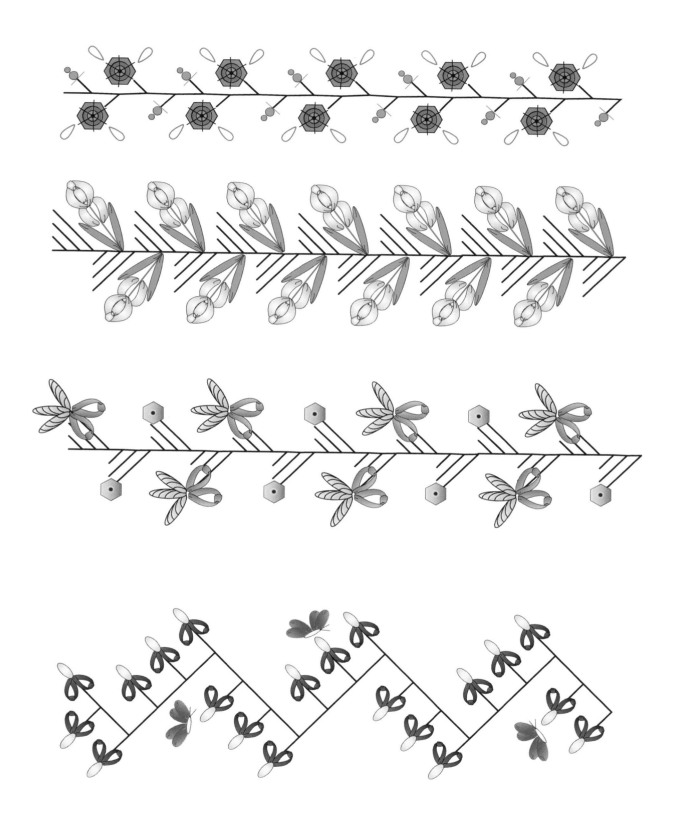

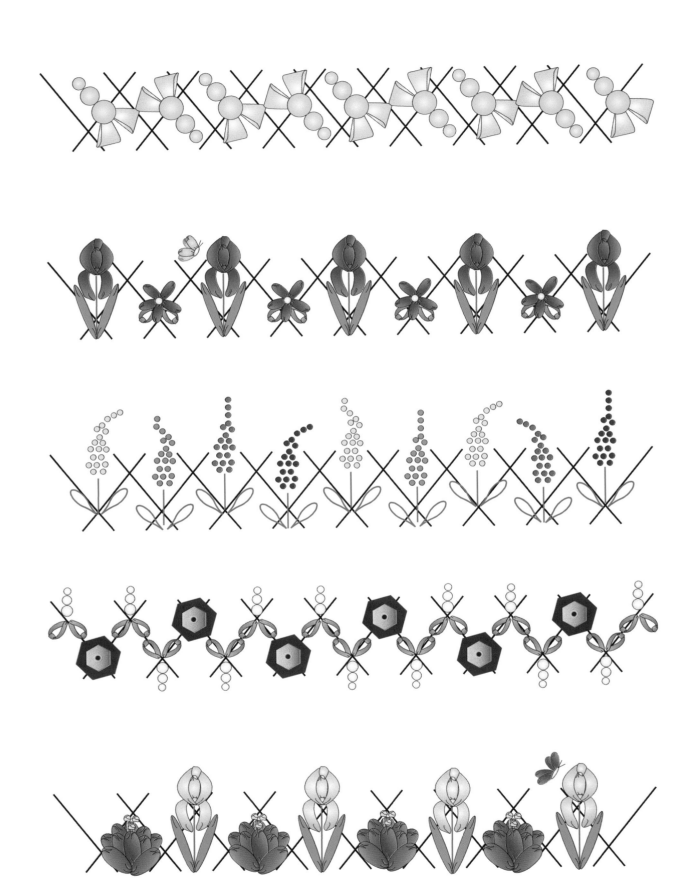

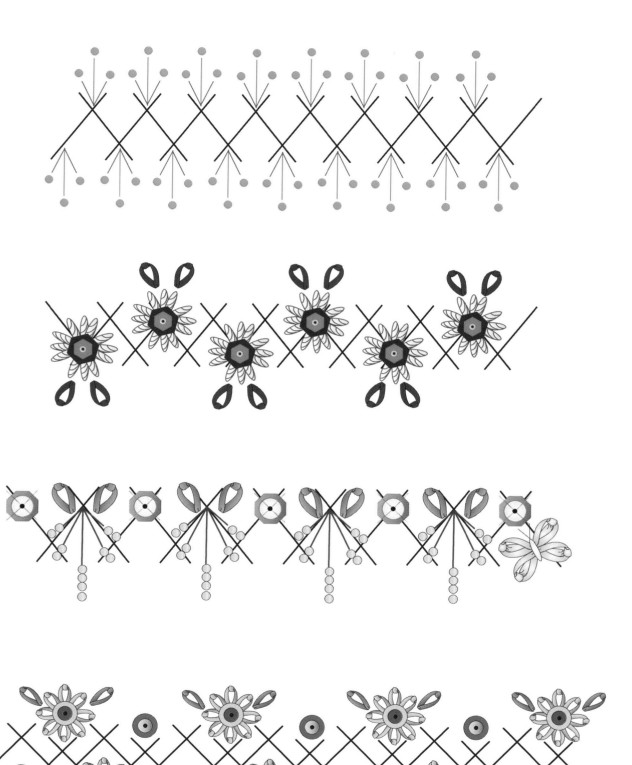

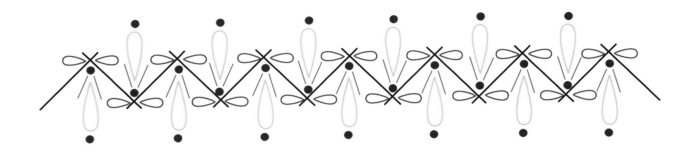

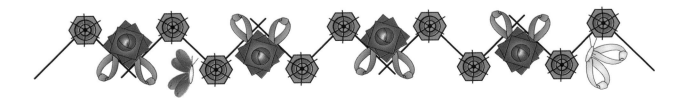

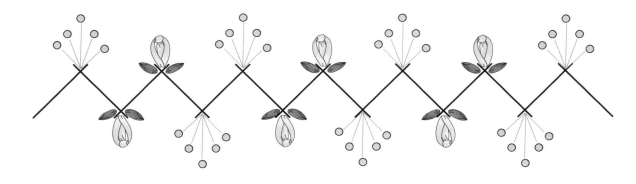

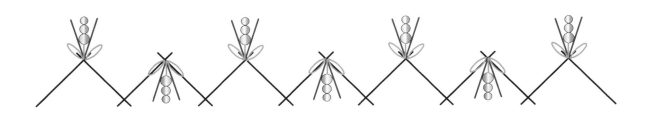

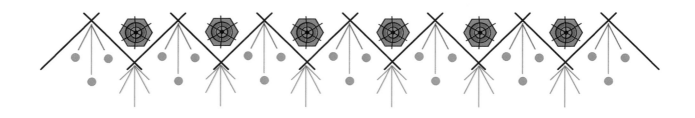

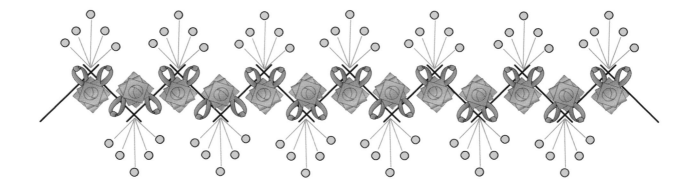

44

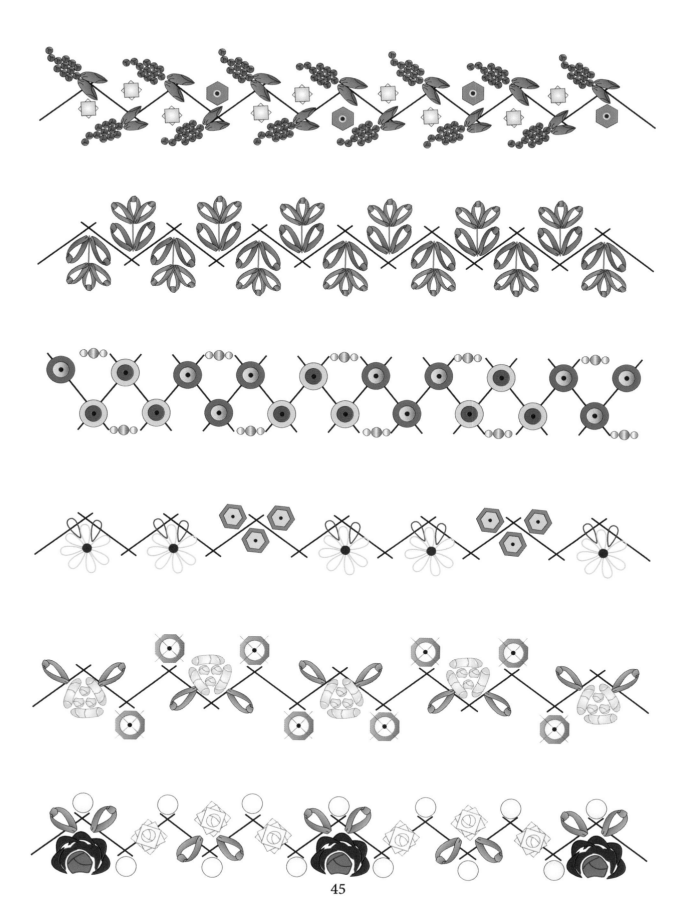

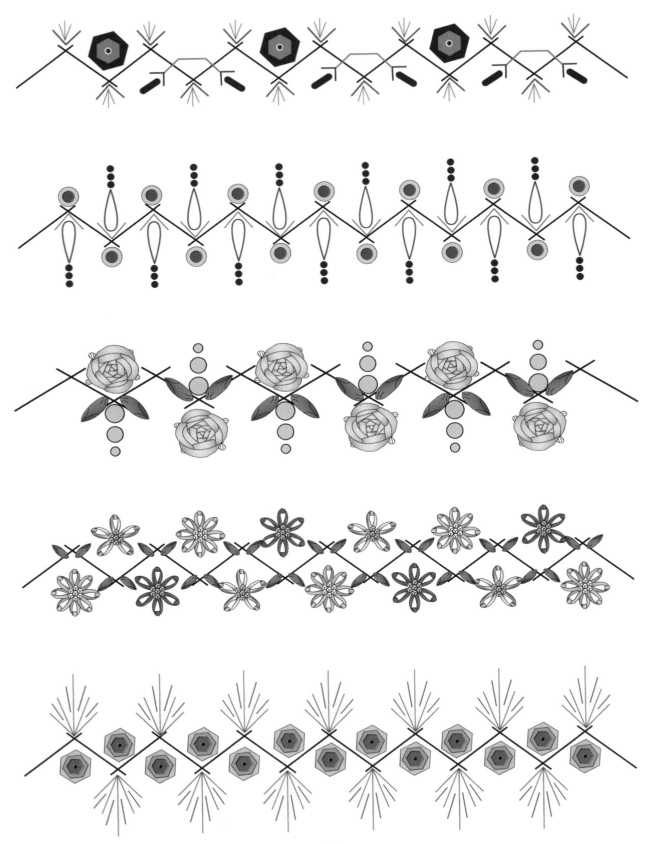

46

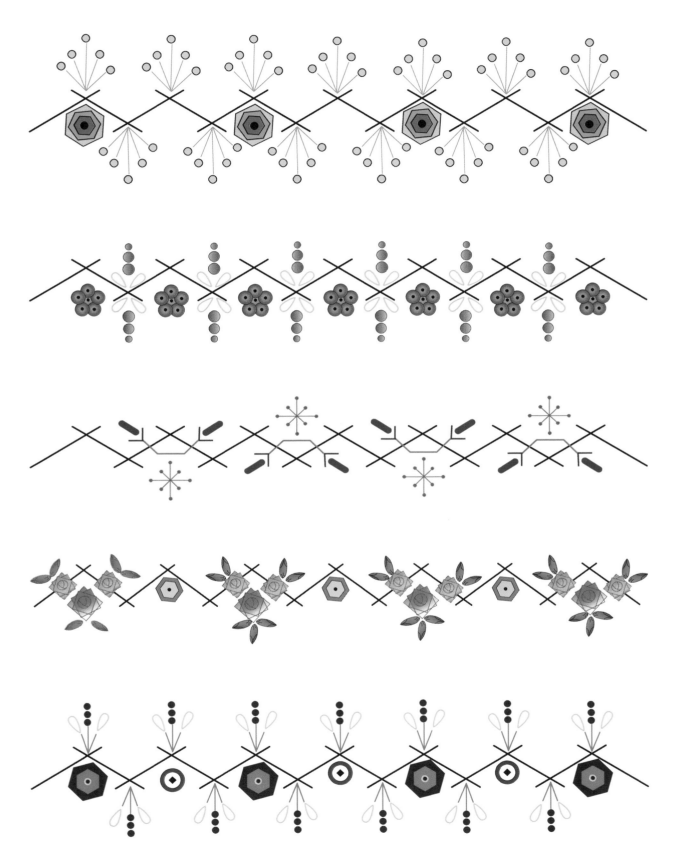

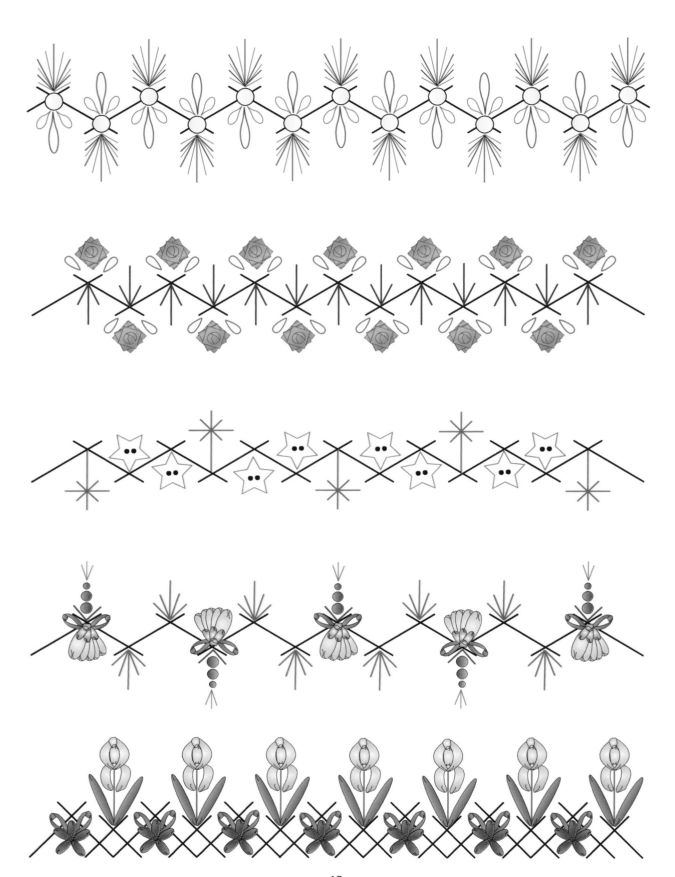

49

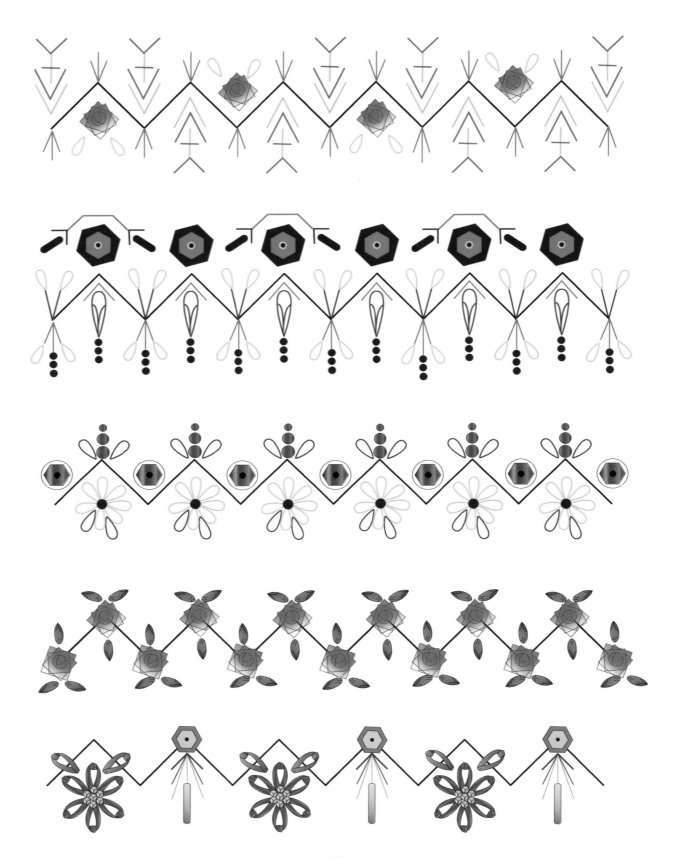

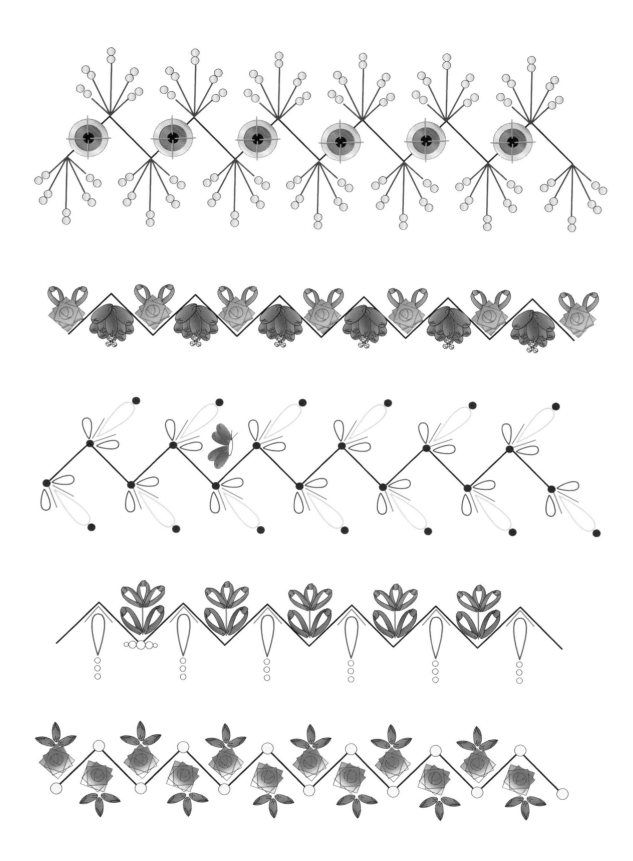

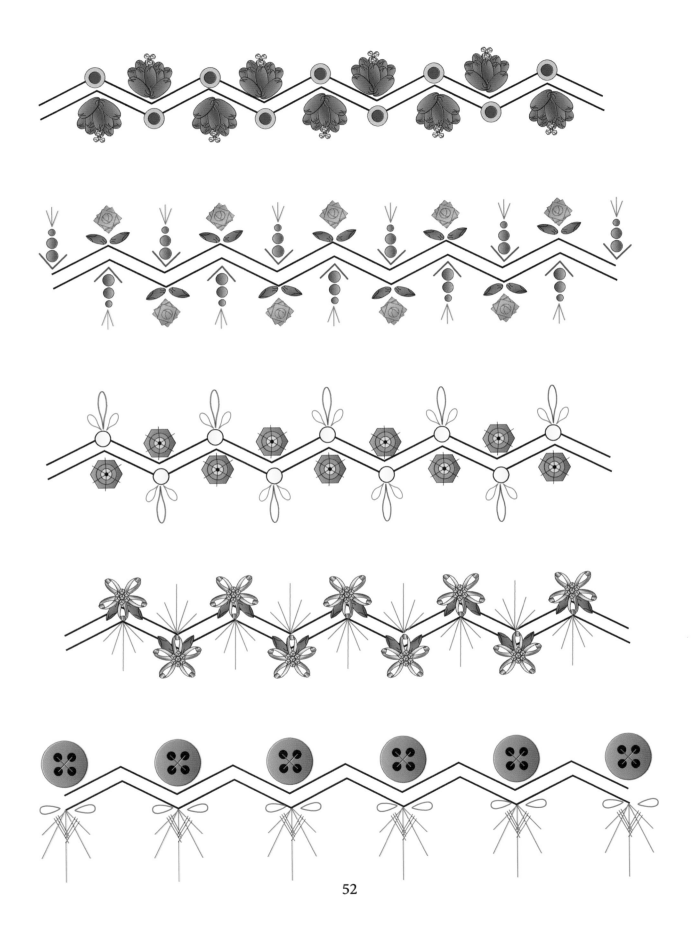

53

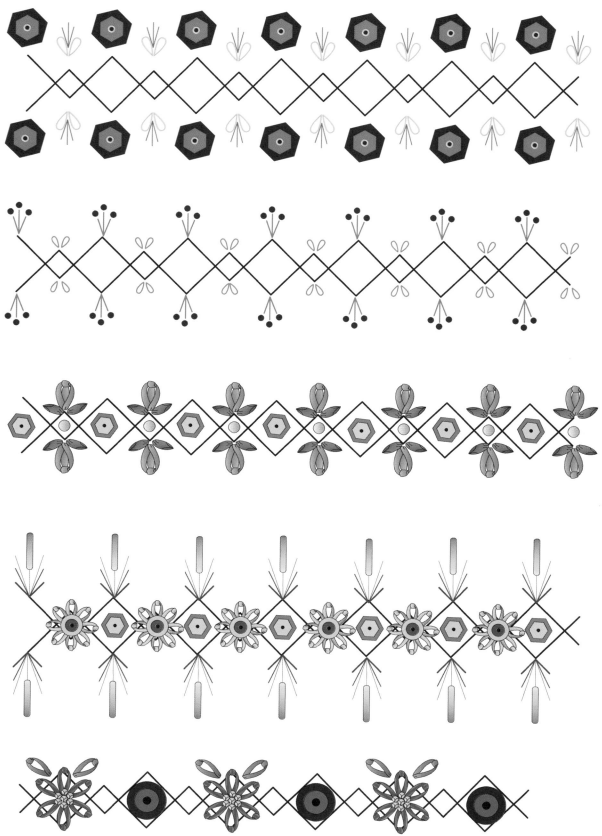

59

Shape Template Seam Designs

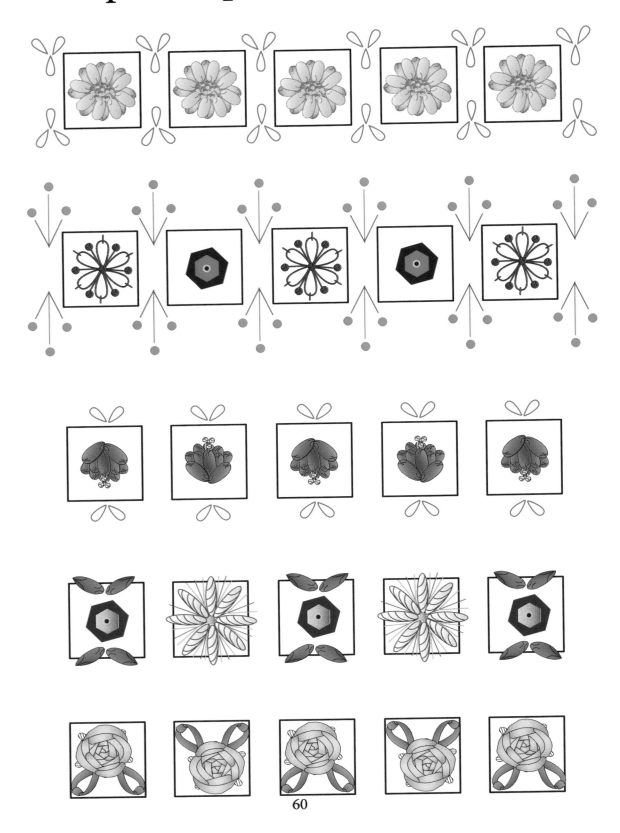

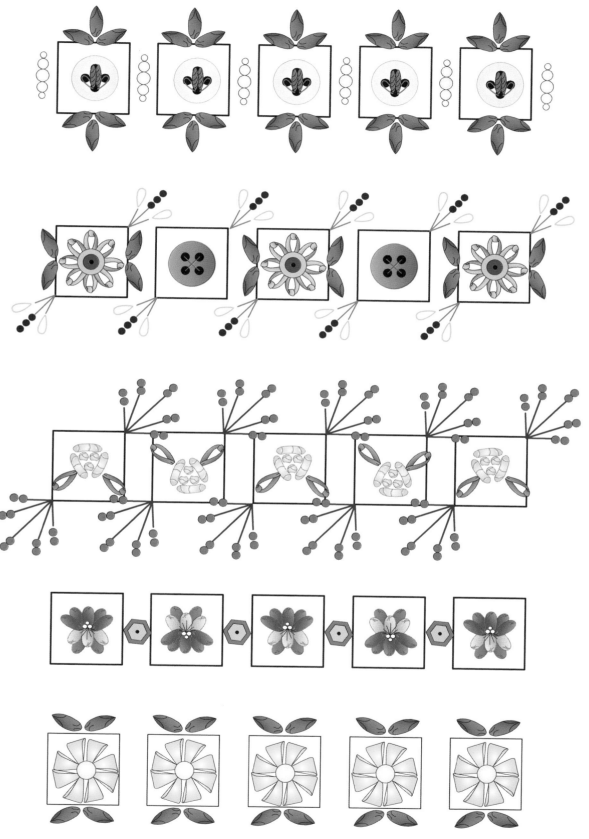

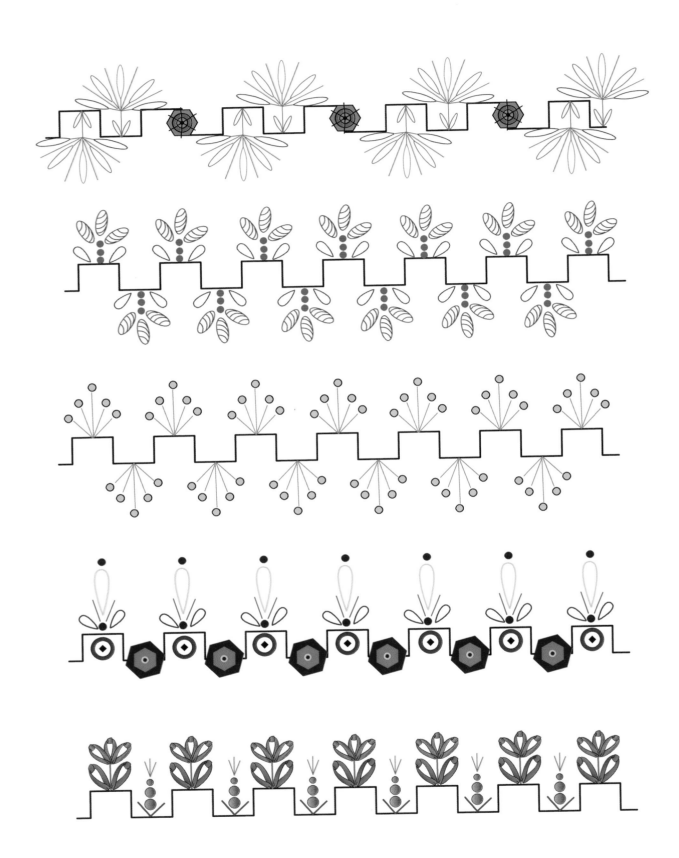

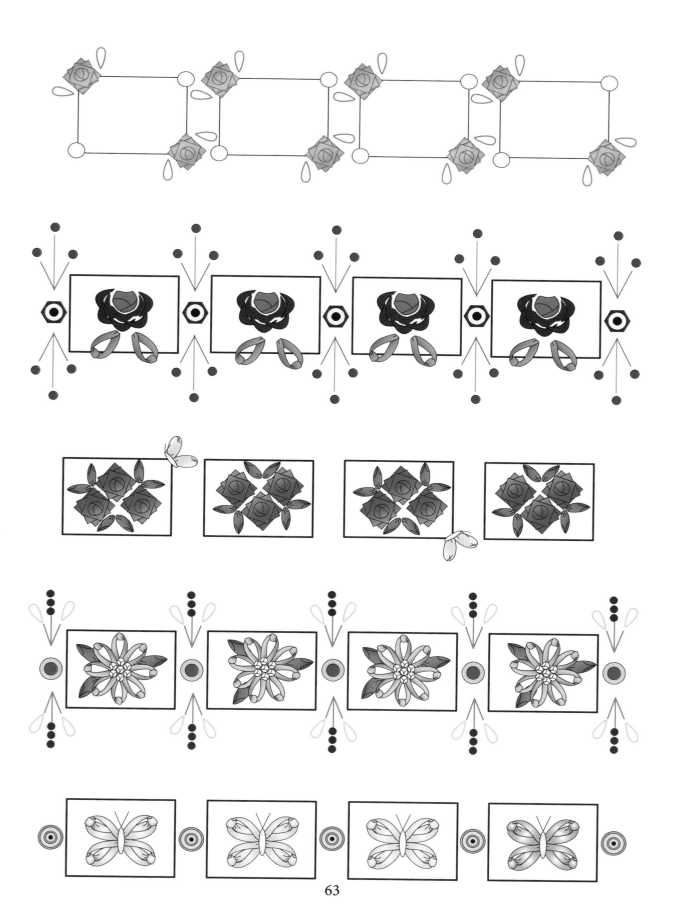

63

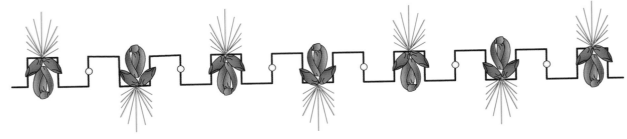

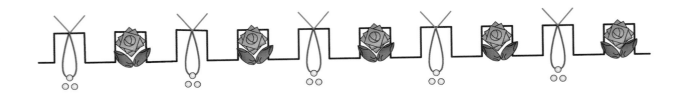

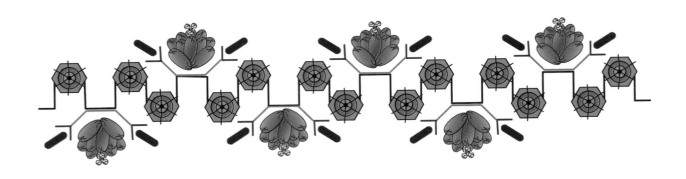

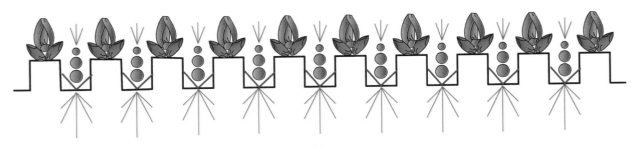

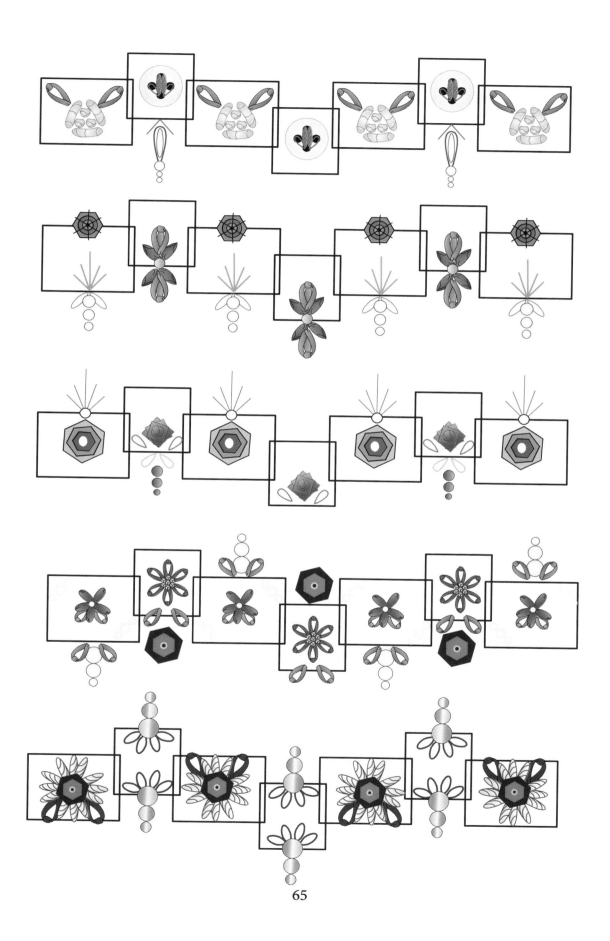

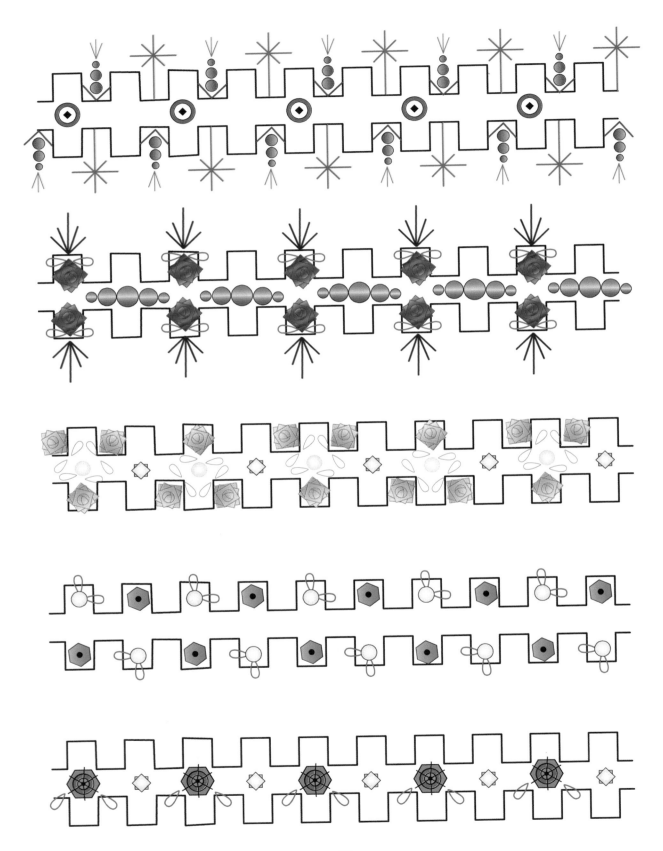

66

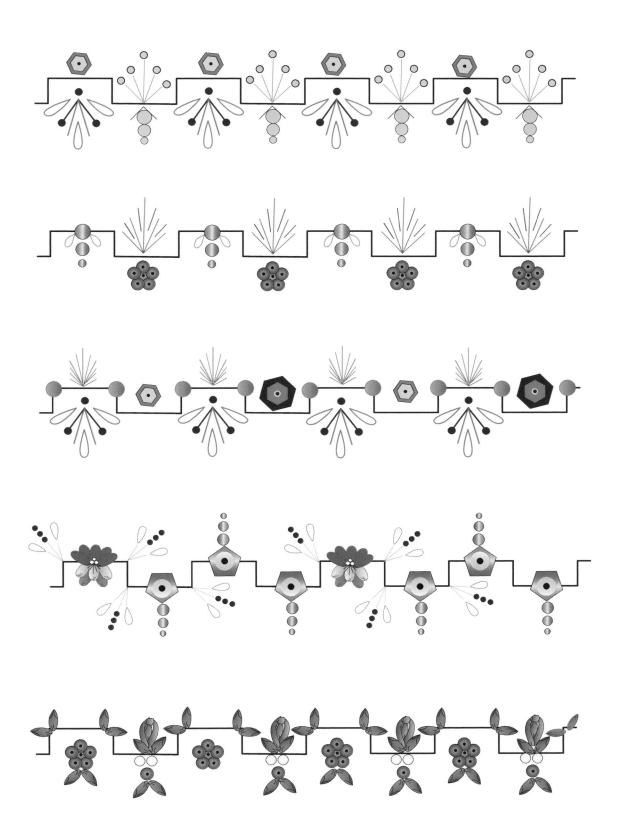

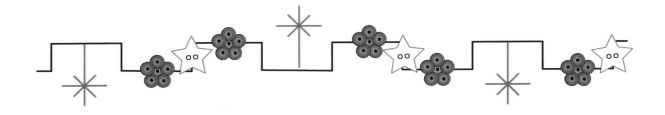

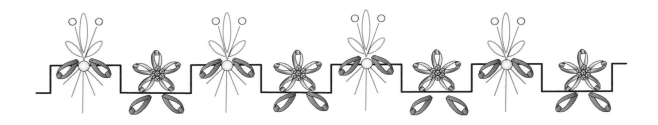

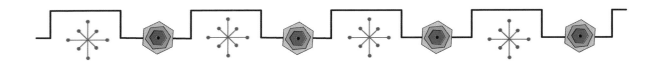

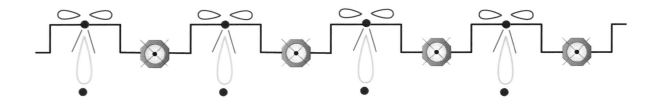

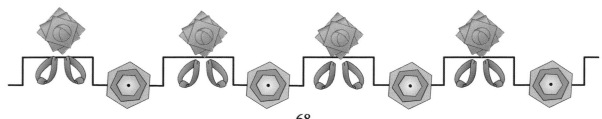

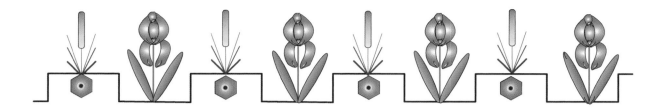

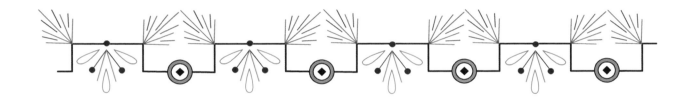

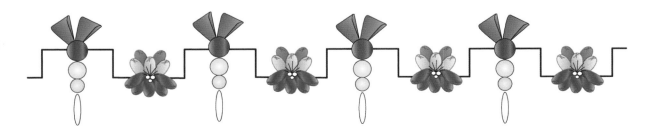

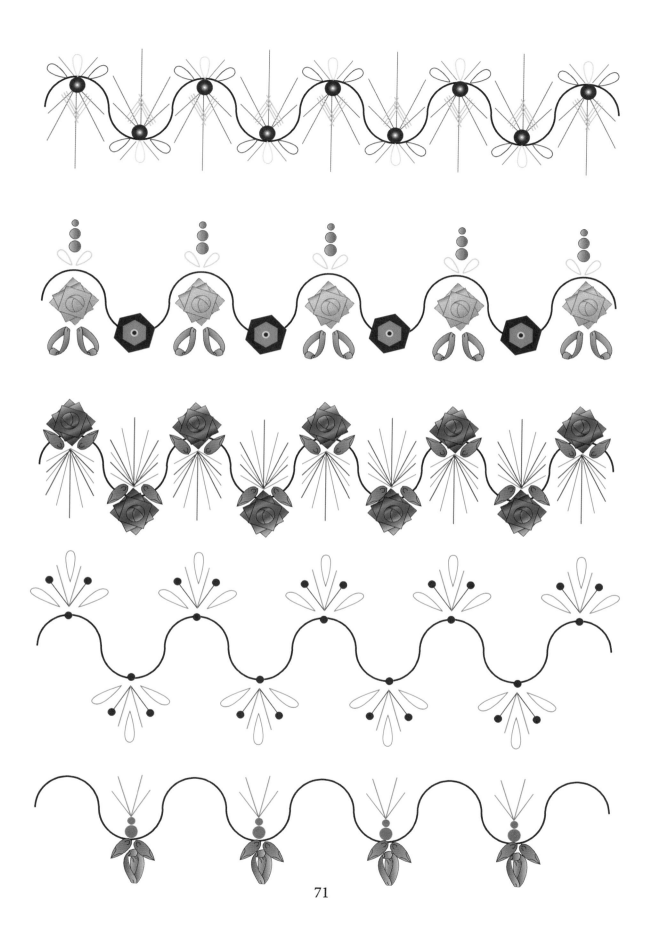

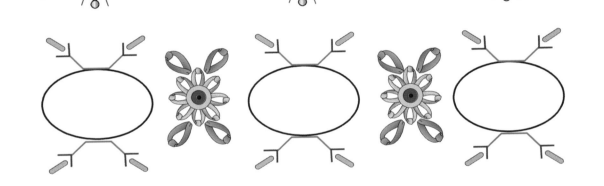

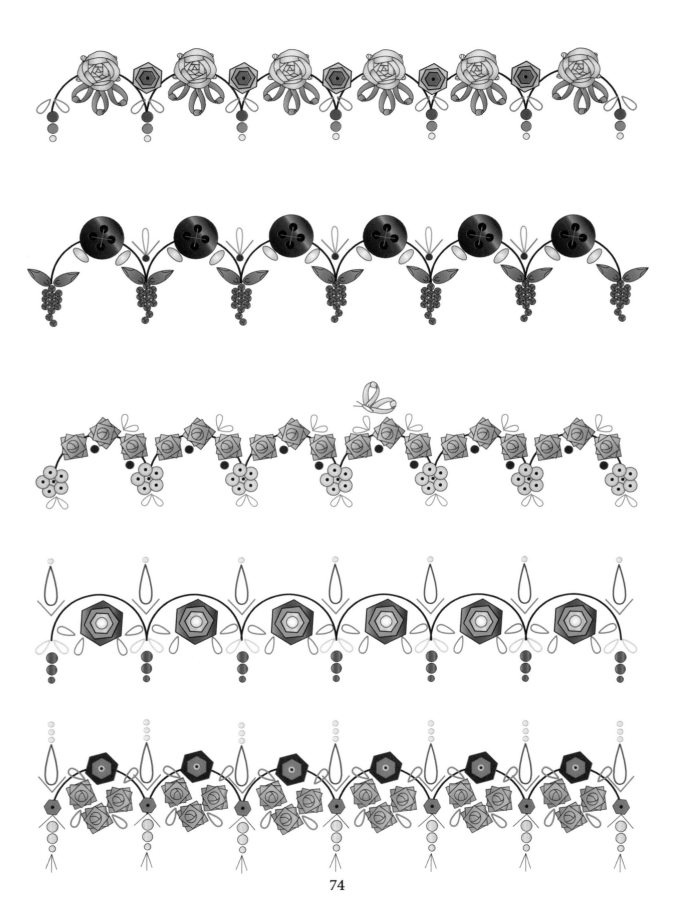

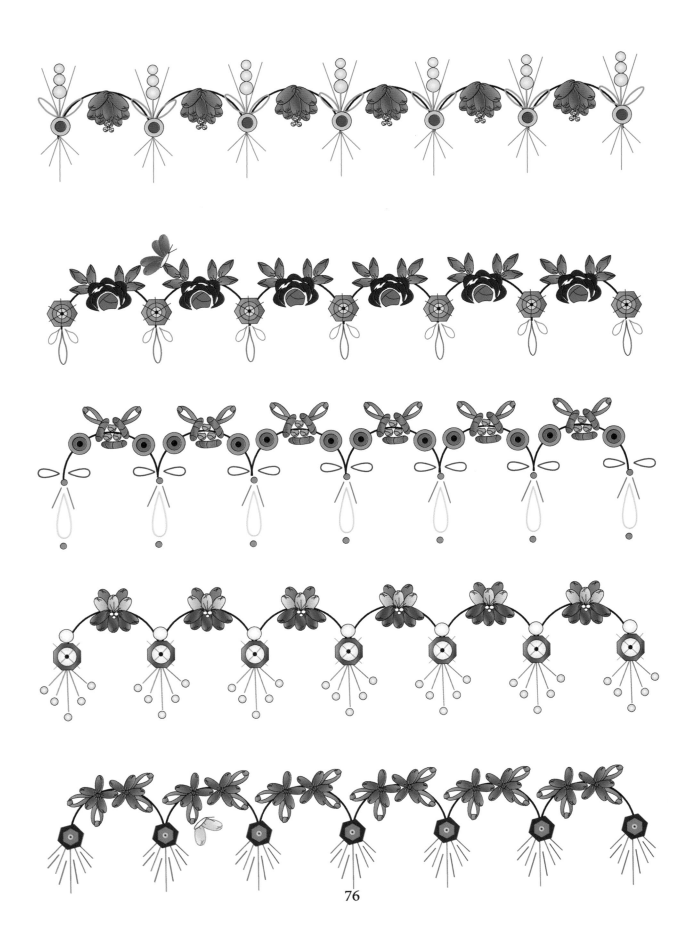

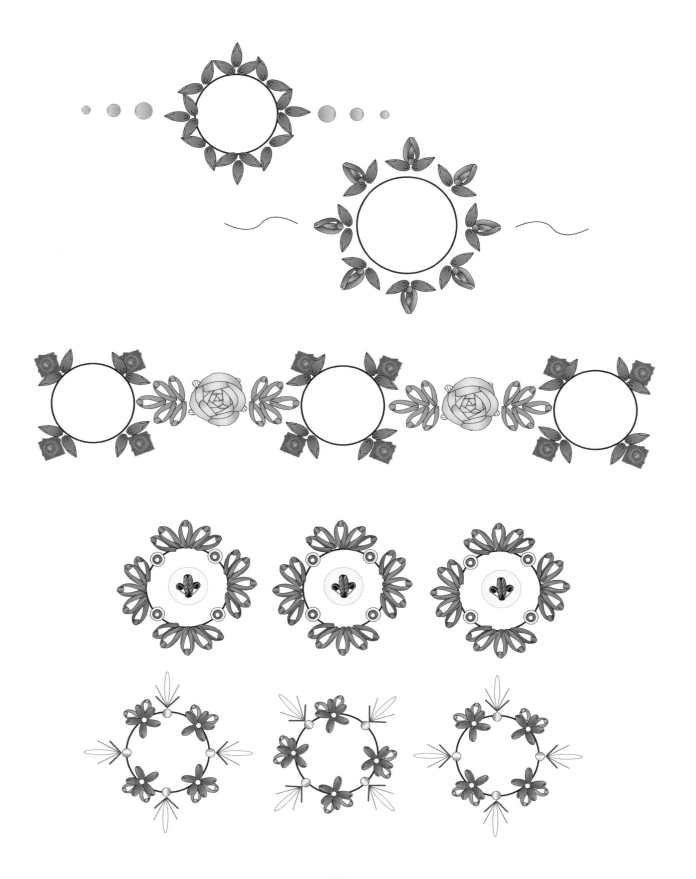

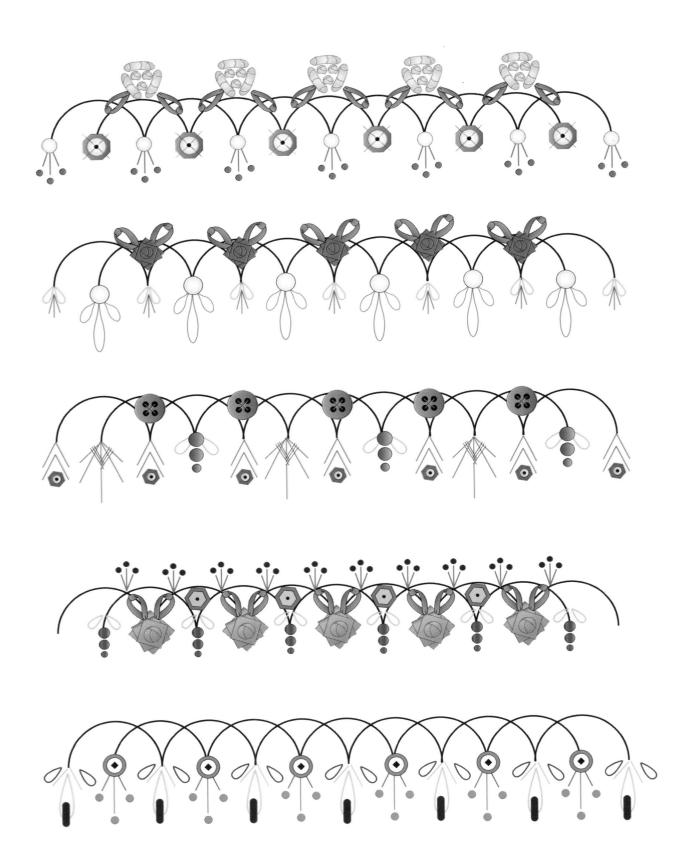

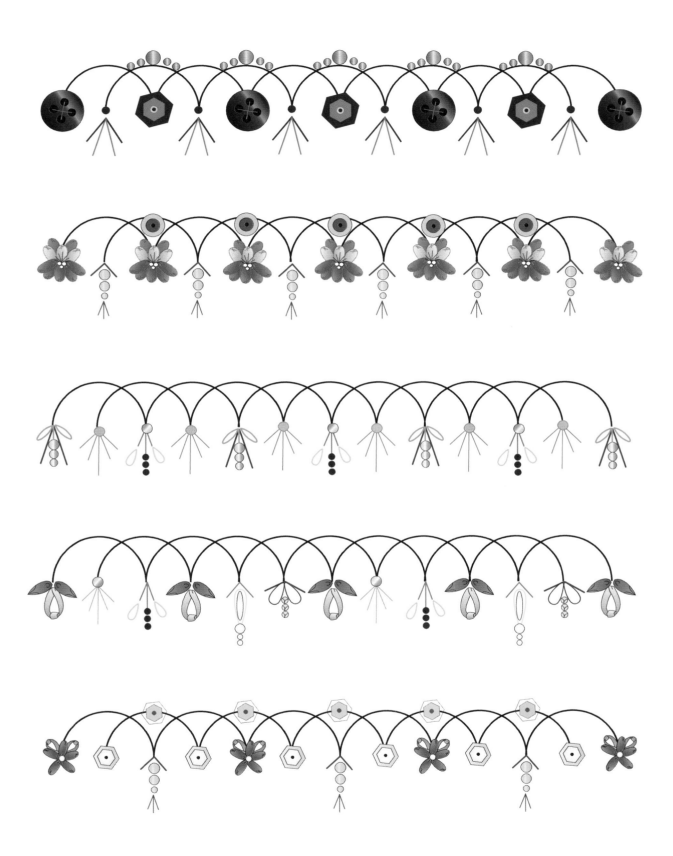

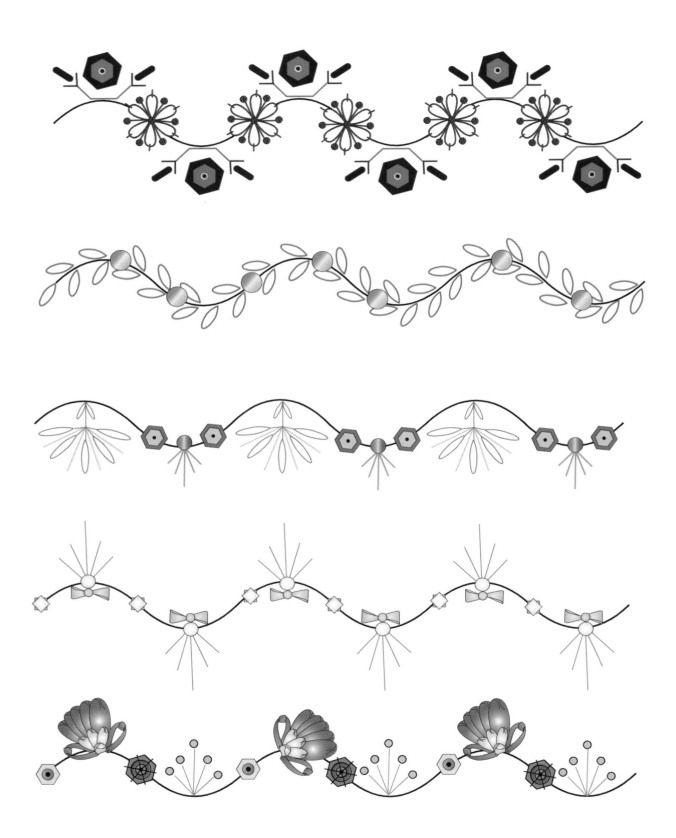

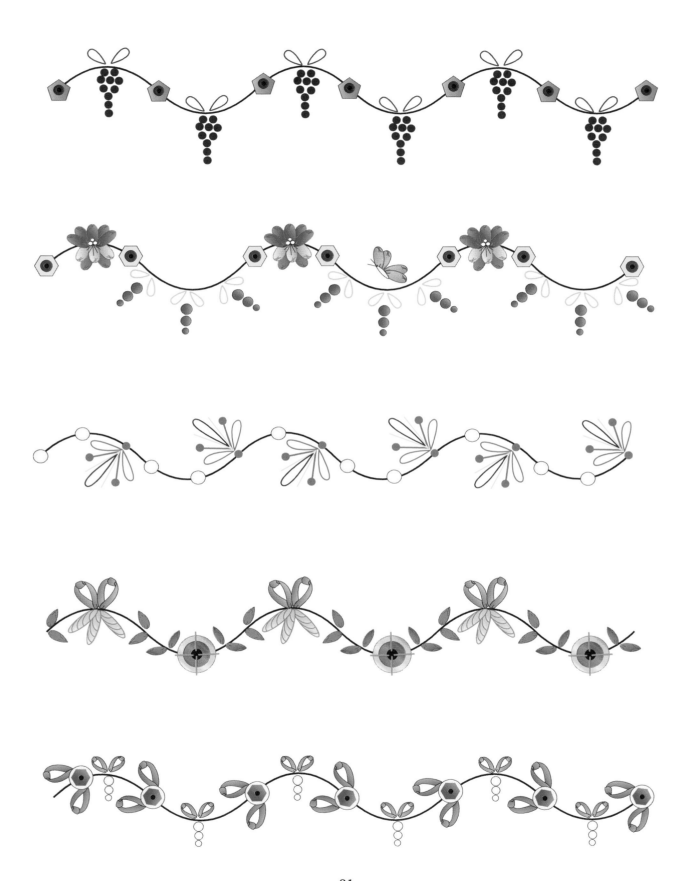

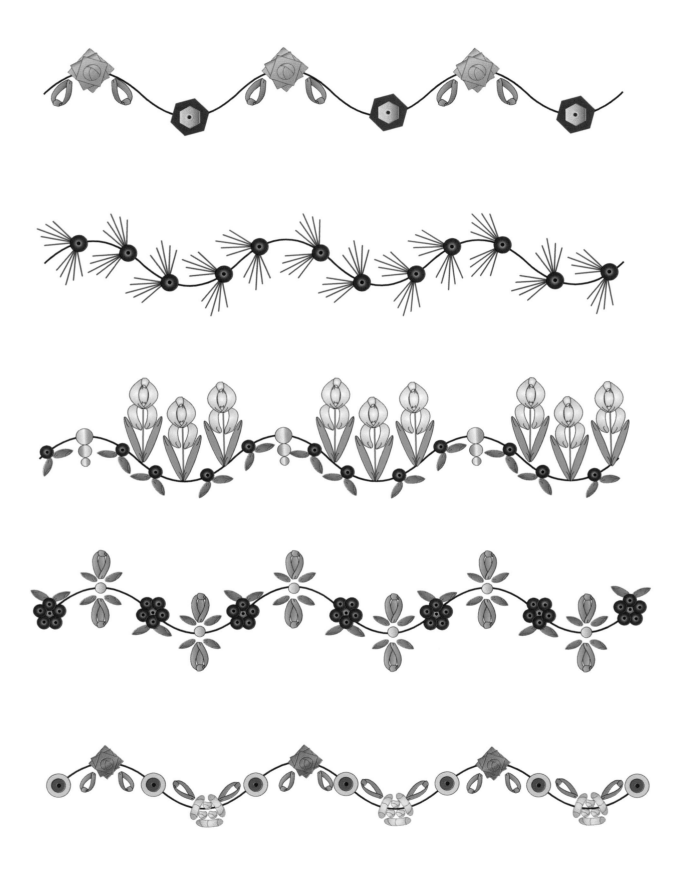

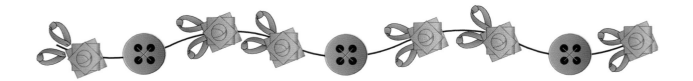

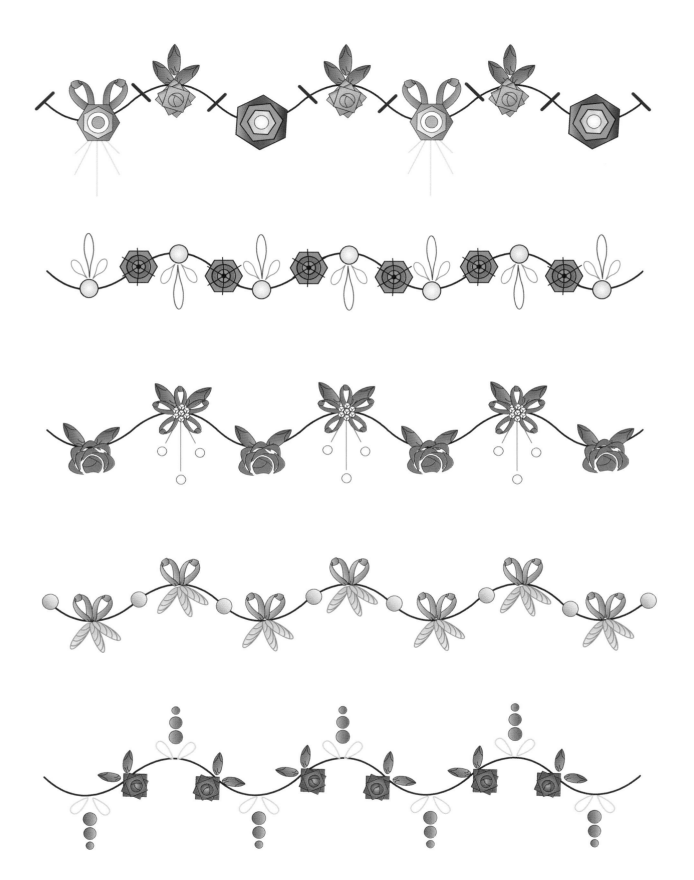

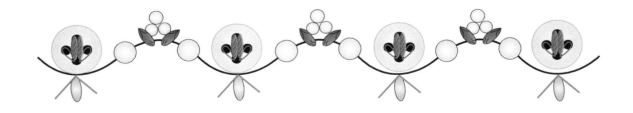

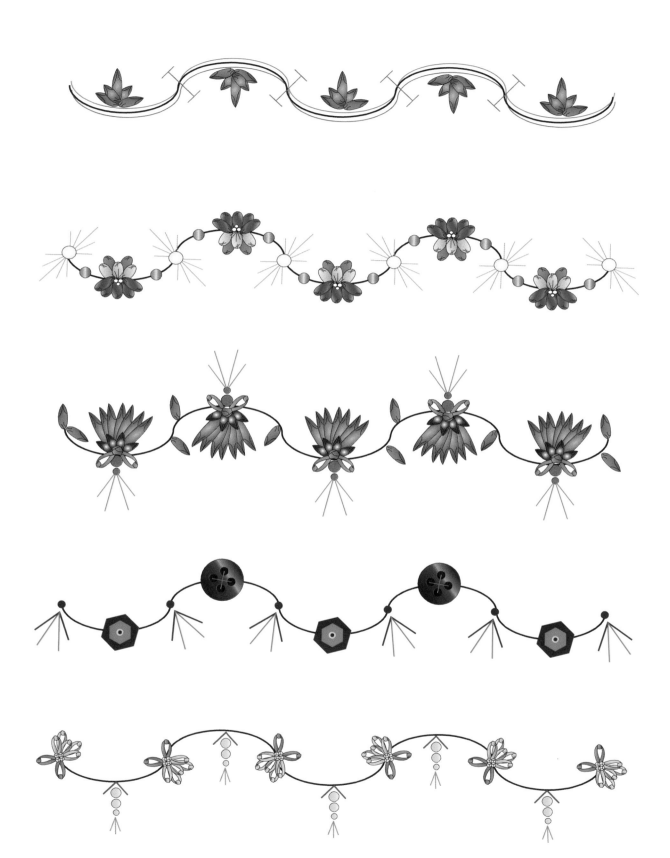

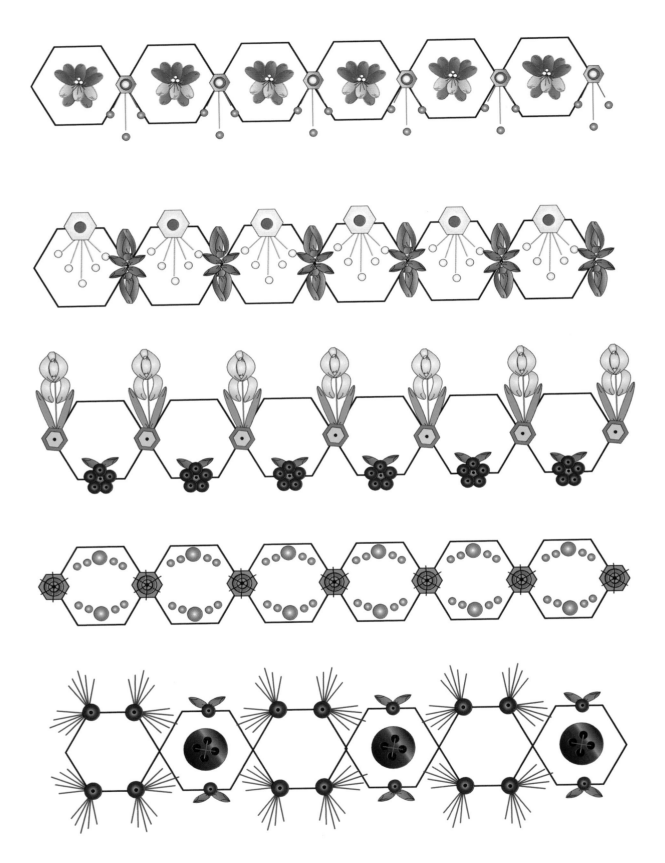

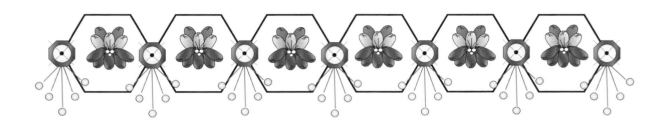

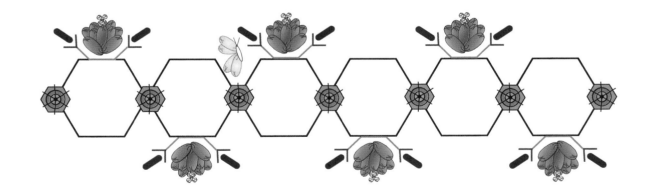

92

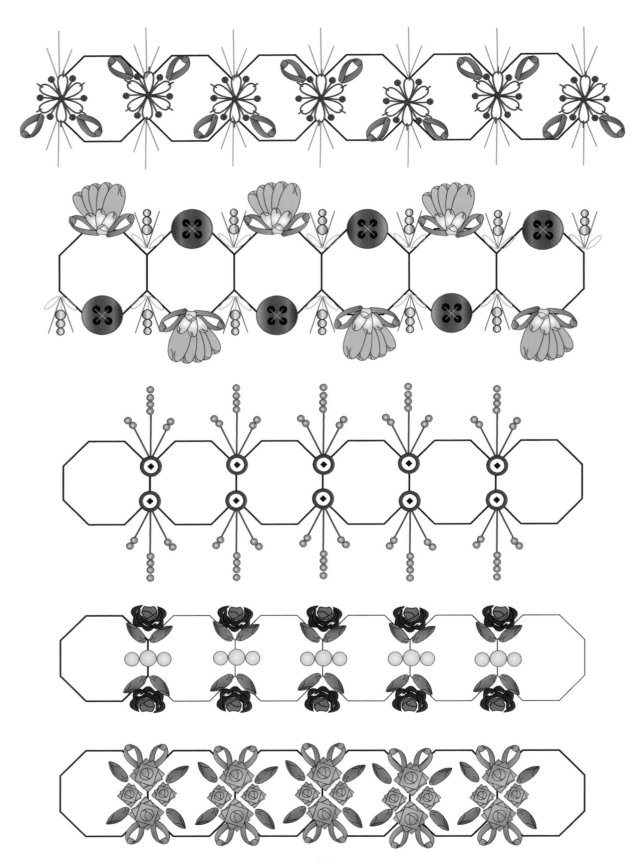

94

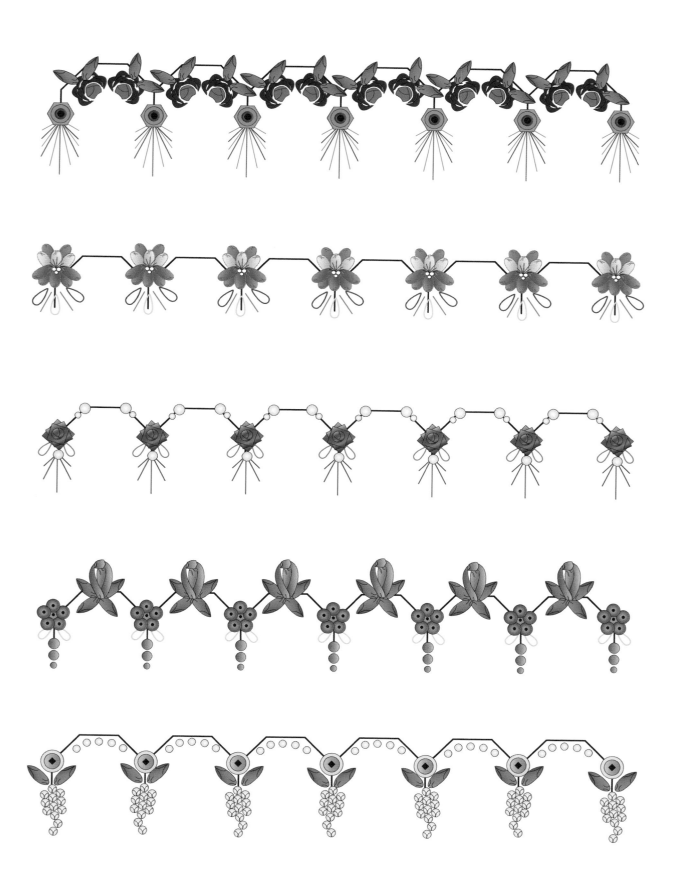

95

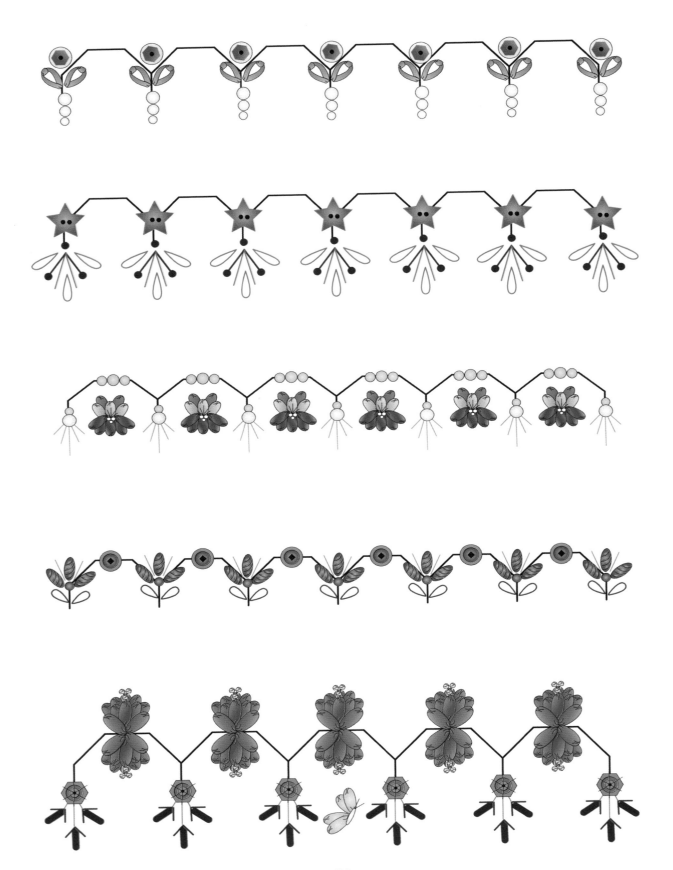

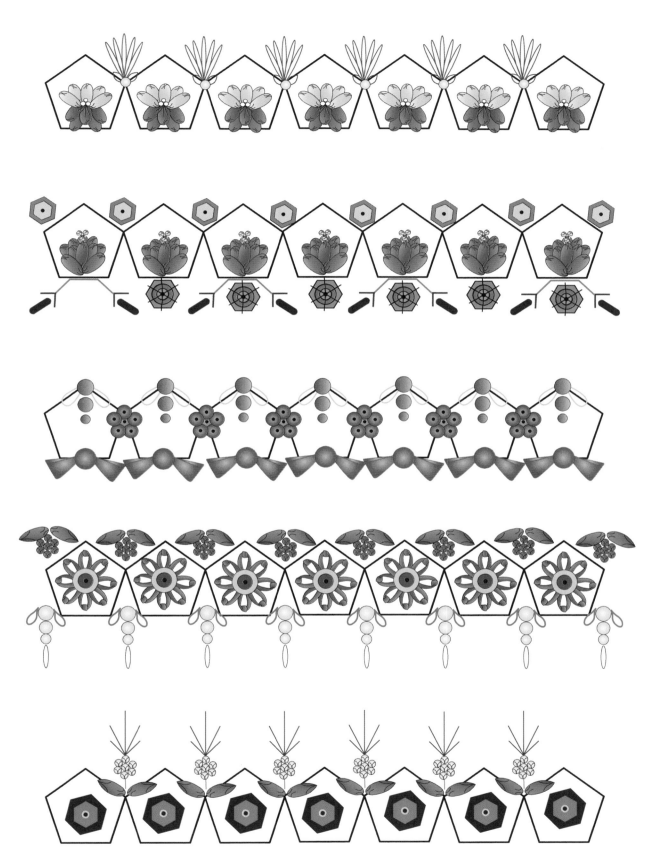

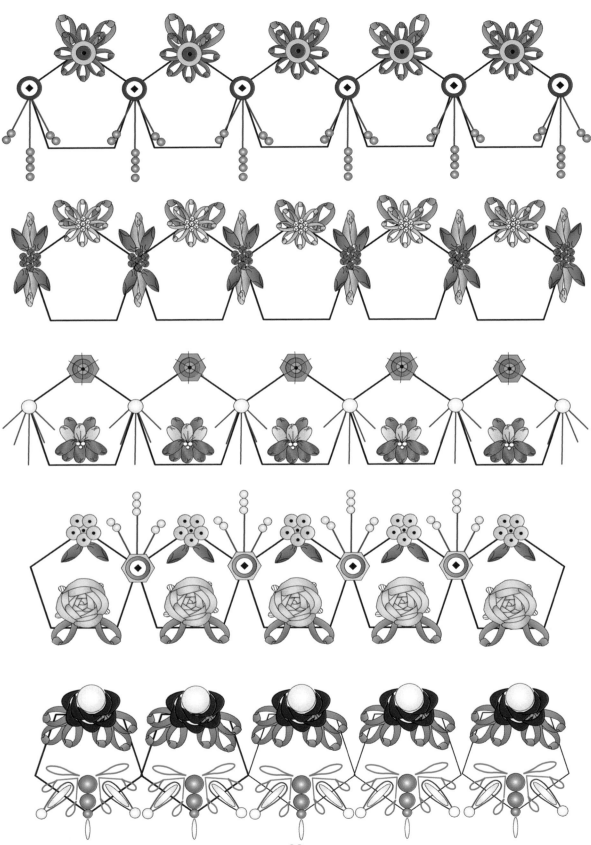

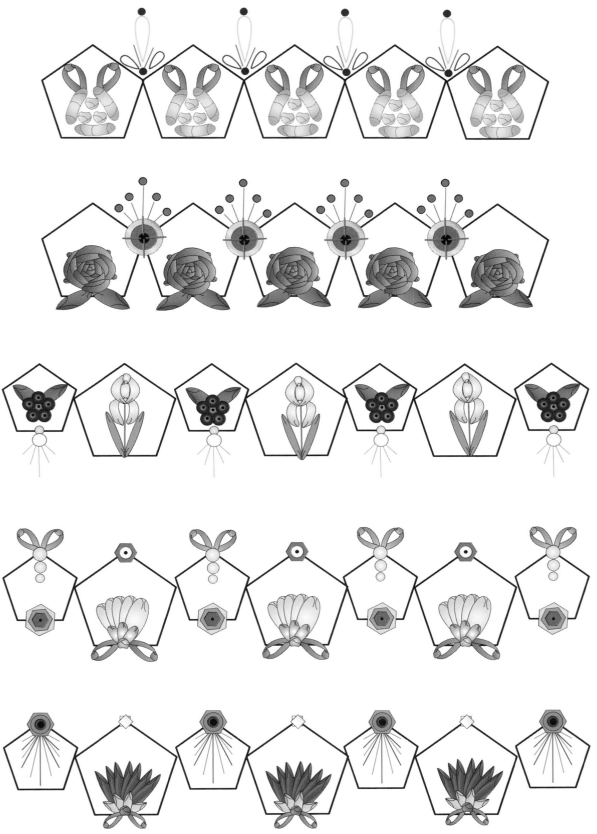

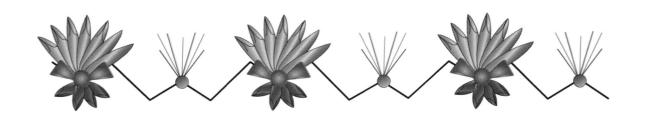
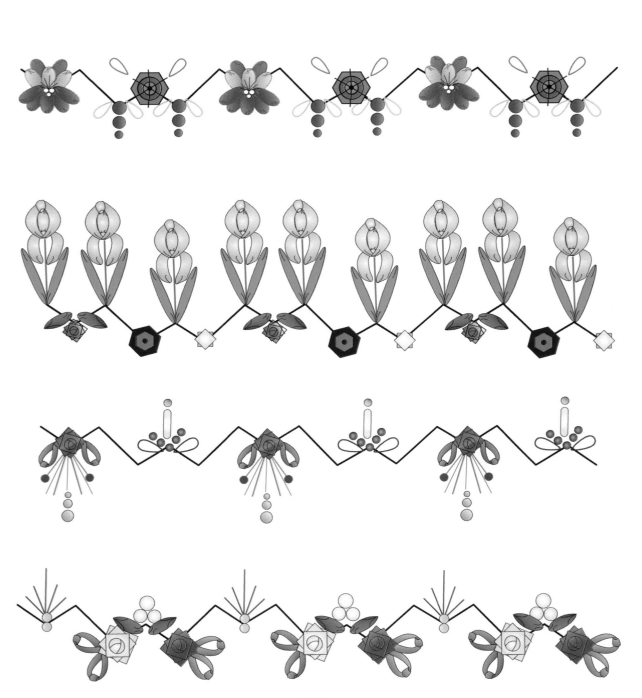

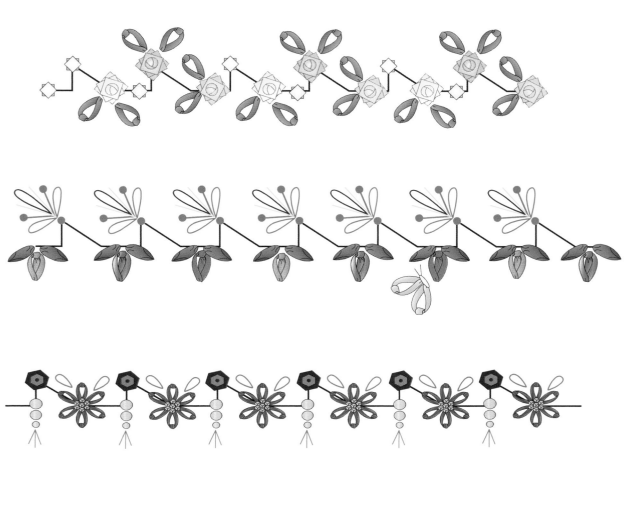

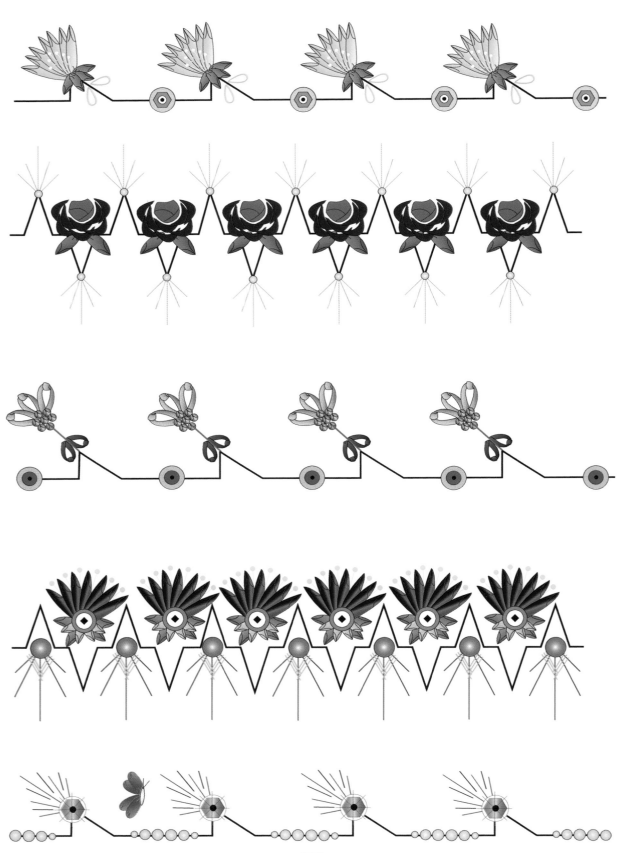

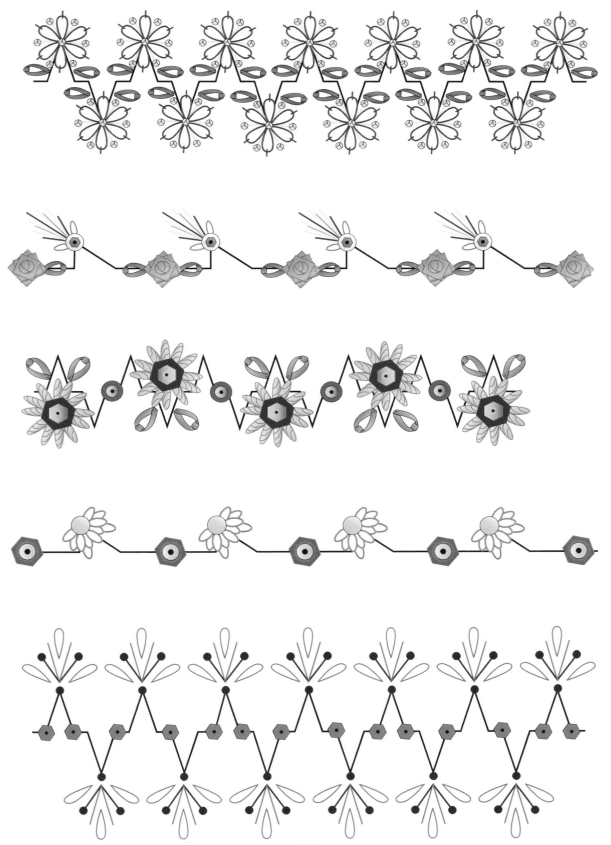

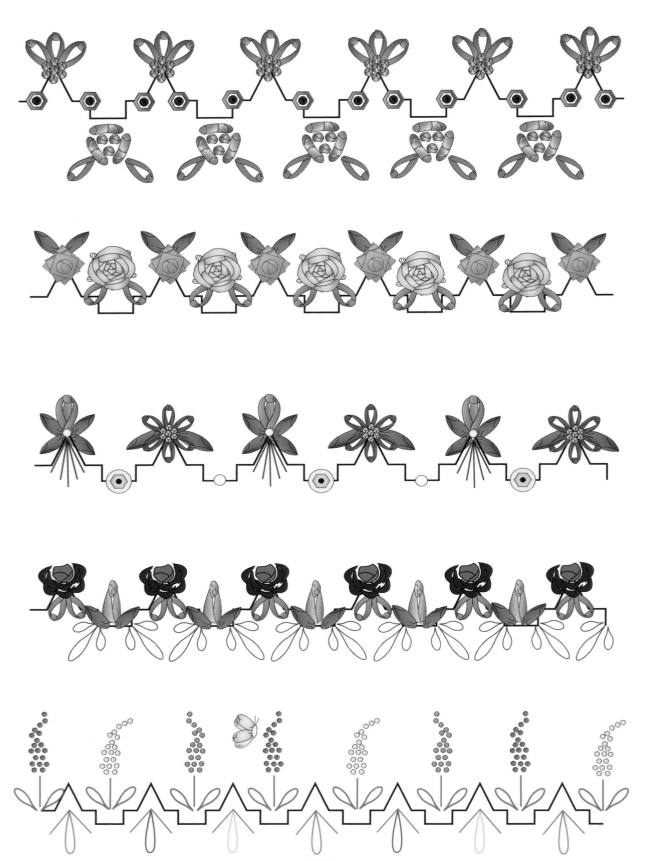

105

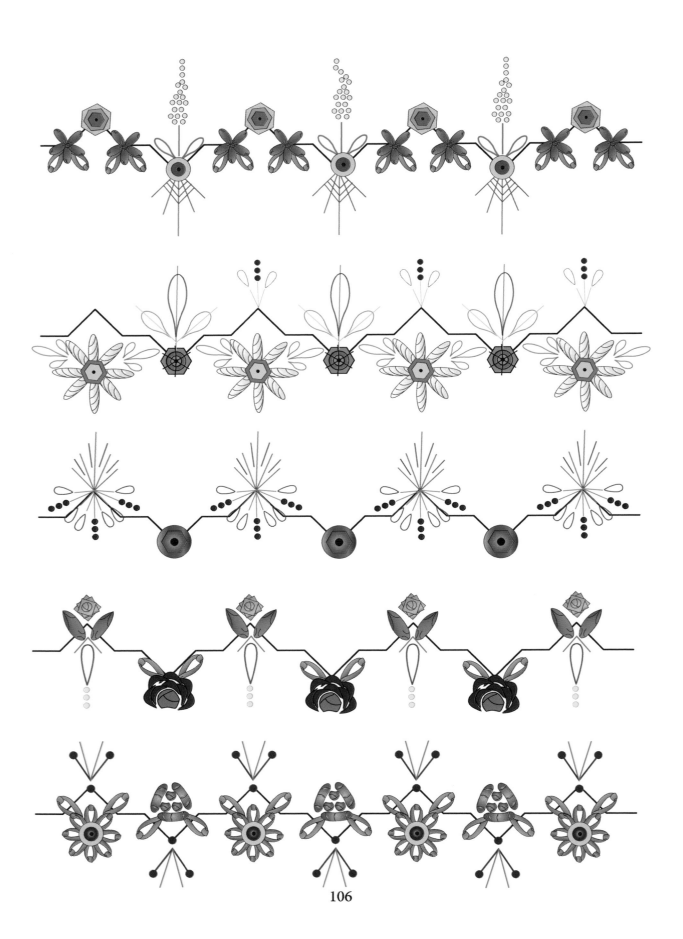

106

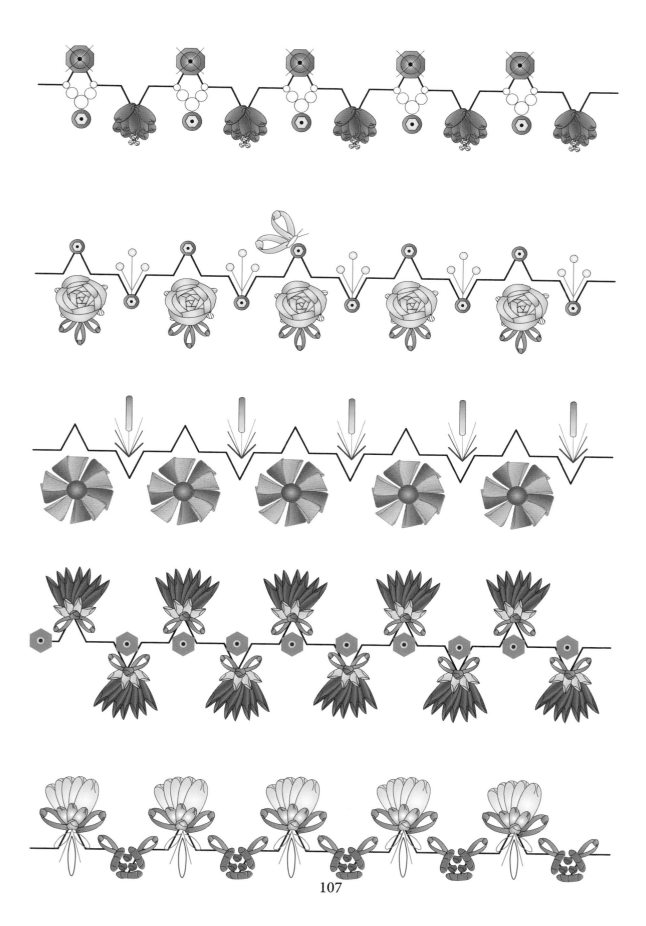

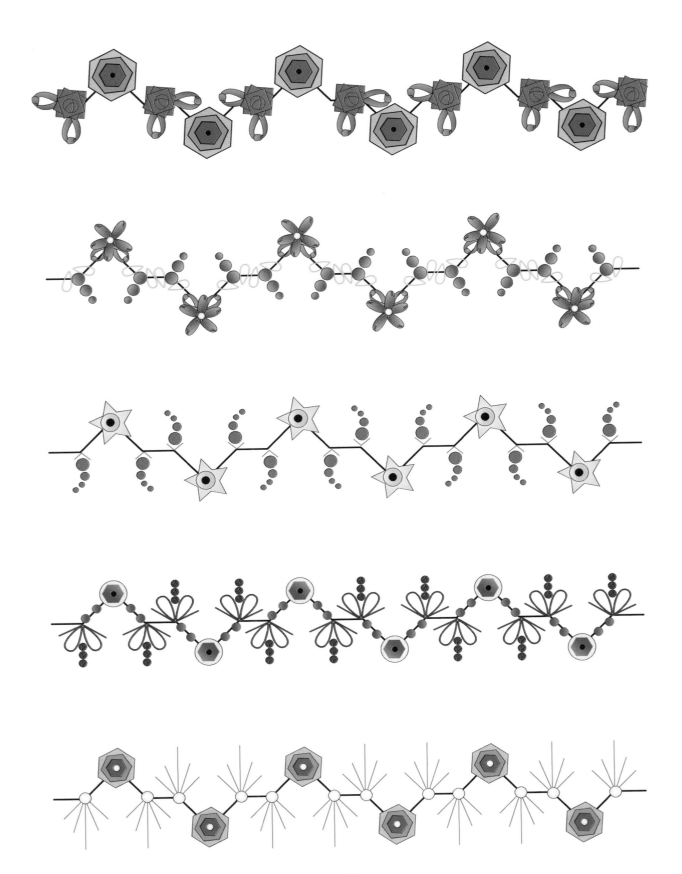

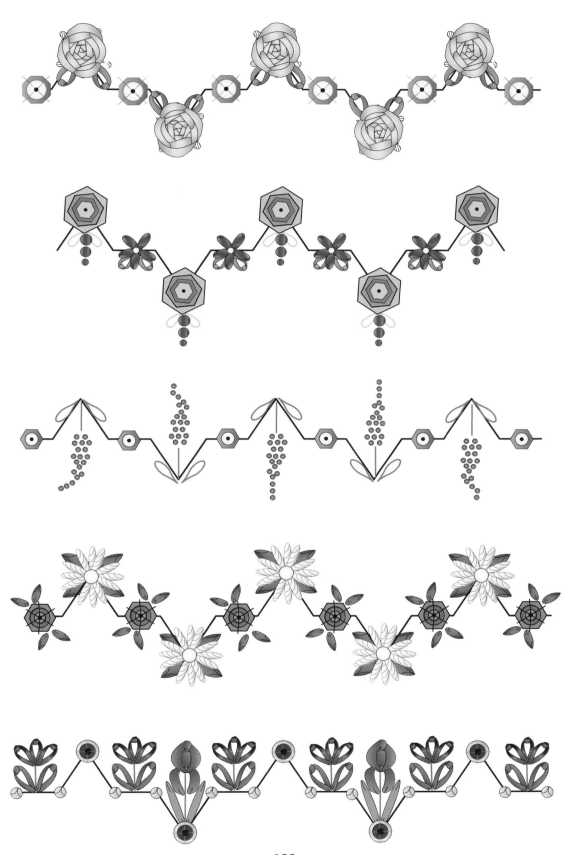

109

Creating & Using Templates

TEMPLATES ARE HELPFUL to keep embroidery stitches uniformly spaced and aligned along a sewn seam between patches of fabric. The result is a neat, uniform, and beautifully embellished seam.

There are several types of templates available today. Most are open grids or shapes. To my knowledge (at the time of writing this book) there are no Stitch Templates on the market. I do provide these as part of my courses on the Shawkl.com blog. I've been designing, printing, and making my own templates for about five years now. So, I'm going to show you how to make your own.

All of the seams in this book correspond to a template for the Base Seam (shown in black ink for all seams). However, you do not have to create templates to use these seam designs. Just free-hand embroider your basic seam and then add the other stitches and embellishments layered on top just as the specific seam design shows. There are two types of templates in this book: STITCH and SHAPE.

STITCH TEMPLATES -- A Stitch Template is a diagram of a specific embroidery stitch, like the Herringbone Stitch. On the template, the stitch is drawn to scale with "dots" placed at the Needle UP and Needle DOWN position locations. These dots are punched out in the template, leaving little holes.

Herringbone

When the template is lain on top of the crazy patch block, aligned with a sewn seam,

these little holes are places to put a marking instrument. A standard pencil for example, can be used to mark a tiny "dot" on the fabric where each hole in the template is located.

Once the Base Seam has been marked using a template, the embroidery work is done in the normal way. The marked dots provide a guide for placement of the needle to go UP or DOWN as the specific embroidery stitch is created.

SHAPE TEMPLATES -- A Shape Template is a solid template that can be traced around. A circle or square for instance is a shape template. More complex shapes are also possible, by adding gentle curves, half circular shapes (like bumps) or sharp peaks/valleys. These shapes are connected to form a line of repeated shapes... like a row of circles for example.

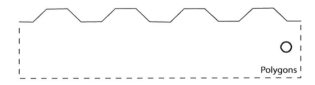
Polygons

Instead of dots to mark the needle position, the "edges" of the template shape is traced along using your choice of marking instrument. I like to use a standard #2 pencil for light fabrics and a white chalk pencil for dark fabrics. If you have issues marking on the front of your fabrics, you can flip a crazy quilt block over and mark along the seam reflected on the foundation fabric. The result of marking along a shape template is a solid line marked on the fabric rather than a grouping of dots.

Any embroidery stitch that can be sewn along a line can be then created to embellish this marked Base Seam. Some possible embroidery stitches for this purpose include: Running Stitch, Back Stitch, Stem Stitch, Outline Stitch, Chain Stitch, or Blanket Stitch. All of these mentioned are simple basic embroidery stitches. Any embroidery book or on-line resource can easily teach you how to create these. Then, all you need to do is stay on the line you just marked on your fabric to create a neat and beautiful beginning for your SHAPE Templated seam. If you more skilled in embroidery, then experiment with different and more complex stitches to use with these templates.

Creating Templates:

You probably already have some shape templates without even thinking of them. A spool of thread for instance can easily become a guide to draw circles along a seam line. That spool becomes a template!

The Template Designs included in this section need to be re-produced on clear plastic or opaque vellum so that you can see through them to align the templates on your fabric seam. You can also reinforce these templates with clear contact paper, laminate sheets, or even clear packing tape. Copy the pages directly to vellum OR scan/save the pages and then print them on plastic or vellum.

Be careful when purchasing your plastic/vellum sheets to ensure you get the type made for your specific printer. Test one page before trying to print several as well. I purchase a small package (25 sheets) of 29-lb clear translucent vellum measuring 8.5" x 11.0" from ThePaperMillStore.com and it works great in my printer. Vellum can also be purchased at most office supply or scrap-booking supply stores. When selecting your vellum sheets, get an opaque variety so that you can see your fabrics when the templates are placed on top of them.

You may think that vellum is not sturdy enough for templates; after all, it is simply paper. However, I created a set of vellum templates for my use in 2013 and am still using them today... and none have torn yet. As you can see from this photo, I have them on a ring for organization. They stay on my desk in a cup; along with my seam ripper, awl, and needle threader. Each are used over and over for every crazy quilt project.

You can alternately hand-trace the template designs on to plastic using a fine tip permanent marking pen. I sometimes use a plastic tablecloth, plastic shower curtain, or waste plastic scrap for templates.

The seam designs in this book correspond to the type of templates included in the book. However, you can use these design without templating the Base Seam. You can "free hand" embroidery the basic seam, and still embellish it using these seam designs as your guide.

Also, even though the book does include 500 different designs...the true number is limitless! This is because every design is simply "one idea". By changing the seam even slightly...like adding more beads, or less beads...you have a new design. So, consider these seam designs as simply a "starting place" for your own creative spirit.

Instructions:
Step #1
Scan/save/print or Copy/print the template pages from the back of the book. If you prefer, you can also go to shawkl.com and download a PDF file of these template pages (which saves the spine of your book from wearing down).

Step #2
Obtain a 1/16 inch hand held hole punch (I got mine from Hobby Lobby in their scrap-booking section. You can also order them on Amazon.com in this size. Don't use one any larger. If you

can not find a hole punch, you can use a large sharp needle (like a chenille needle). But, believe me, the little hole punch is so much easier!

Step #3
Cut the Stitch Templates apart. Using the hole punch, punch out every "dot" on these.

Step #4
Cut the Shape Templates apart. Cut along the specific shape edge using tiny sharp-pointed scissors. A pair of old embroidery scissors works nicely for this task.

Step #5 (optional)
Punch a hole at the end of each template to be able to hang the set of templates from a ring.

Note: If you are concerned about the wear-ability of the templates, you can reinforce the individual templates with clear masking tape. Do this before you punch any holes or cut completely out. Another option is to cover the printed vellum sheet with clear contact paper or laminate it before cutting the templates apart. This will make punching the holes for the Stitch Templates a bit more difficult, but not impossible. Create a few templates and then rest your wrist and shoulders.

Using Templates:

STITCH TEMPLATES -- These reflect some easy to create embroidery stitches (Chevron, Creten, Feather, Herringbone and Straight Stitch) by first marking the needle up/down positions within each stitch design directly to the fabric of your crazy quilt. Each of these Base Seam Stitch Designs can be placed along the center of the sewn patchwork seam or slightly to the left/right. The additional embellishments will cover the seam, even if the template is shifted to either side. This "shifting" is especially helpful to consider when you have wide and thin patches

of fabric seamed together. Shifting towards the wider fabric patch will allow more of the embellishments to fill that space. This helps to balance out the work and prevent multiple seams from crowding each other.

If this is a new concept or is confusing, look at the seam designs on the cover of the book. Pay close attention to the base seams shown in black ink, almost all of these are NOT centered on the seam (where the two adjacent fabrics meet). But, the finished embellished design appears to be across the seam...since parts of it truly are. You do not have to "center" every embroidery seam you create in a crazy patchwork project.

Usage Instructions:
Step #1:
Place the chosen Stitch Template on top of your sewn seam. (for example, the Chevron Stitch Template). Each stitch template has been drawn in various widths, heights, and angles to give you options. Align the length of the template to best fit the sewn seam. It can be centered or shifted up/down as previously stated.

Hold the template so that it does not slip (if using plastic, tape the template to the fabric) using clear office tape. Using a marking tool (a sharp #2 lead pencil is fine for light fabrics) place the tip into each hole of the template and make a mark on the fabric. With a pencil, this is done by "twisting" the pencil lead into the fabric rather than "drawing" as you would a line.

If you do use a pencil, the markings are permanent. So, sharpen the pencil before (and during) it's use so that the tip is small and making only a very tiny dot. Dull pencils make a large dot that is seen more readily. So, it is in the "wrong place" you will always see it. However, if/when this happens, don't panic; it is simply a design opportunity. Place more beads, a tiny butterfly, etc. over this area. But, of course, it is better that you THINK before you mark on your fabric so that your template is aligned properly.

Base Seam (Herringbone Stitch)

Once the template is in place, do not move it around until you have finished marking each of the holes that are over your seam. If the seam is longer than the template, mark all of the shown positions and then shift the template to repeat the rest of the length of the seam. Align it with the prior markings so you keep the same uniform spacing of the marks along the length of the entire seam.

Step #2:
Use the stab method (rather than the scoop method) to embroidery the chosen stitch along the seam if you are using a hoop.

Note: I strongly recommend hooping your work. There is even a set of instruction on the shawkl. com blog for building your own hoops; just check under the Tutorials Tab and scroll down until you see those instruction links.

Use the dots to guide your needle's up/down positions for the specific embroidery stitch you are creating. The stitch is embroidered just as you would without a template...you are just visually guided by the dots as to "where" the needle should be going up/down.

Step #3:
The Base Seam is now finished using the Stitch

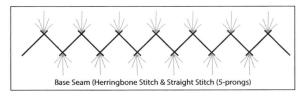
Base Seam (Herringbone Stitch & Straight Stitch (5-prongs)

Template. Next, you can layer other stitches and object on top of this seam to embellish it further. This is done free-hand with the exception of some of the items included in the Object Template. These are just extra small template to help you maintain a constant height and width for some repetitive groups of stitches (mostly Straight Stitches, Detached Chain Stitches, or French/Colonial Knots).

Step #4: (optional)
A favorite Object Template of mine is the 5-prong fan. It can be used to mark only 3 prongs as well, just skip the #2 and #4 prongs in the design. Many of the designs in the book will use this template so it is good to practice with it.

Also, note the position of these extra stitches in the designs. For example, when adding beads the seam design may include "space" between the Base Seam and the other parts of the design. So, an Object Template (like the 5-prongs) may need to be placed slightly above each of the "bars" of the Chevron Stitch rather than right on that bar line before you mark the dots on your fabric. This would leave room for a sequin/bead to later be sewn in this space...and NOT cover up the 5-prong too much.

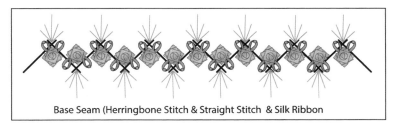
Base Seam (Herringbone Stitch & Straight Stitch & Silk Ribbon

When stitching the 5-prong, begin at the furthest point of the center prong by needling up. Then needle down at the base of the 5-prong group, this is a simple Straight Stitch. Next, we complete the two outer stitches in the same manner; stitching from the outside dot to the base of the prong group. Lastly, create the two remaining Straight Stitches. Now the prong is completely stitched and you can anchor your thread to the back of our work.

After all of the thread embroidery is finished you can add silk ribbon elements, then sequins/beads.

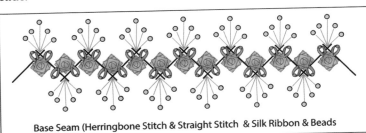
Base Seam (Herringbone Stitch & Straight Stitch & Silk Ribbon & Beads

"Thread" embroidery can be done with floss (2-3 plies), perle cotton, twist, crochet cotton, thin cording, etc. So, don't just limit your work to floss. If you can get it into a needle and pull it through fabric...it is possible to use as a Base Seam "thread".

NOTE: When attaching beads, pass through the individual bead at least twice to secure it. 3-4 passes is even better.

Remember, embellishing is all about layering. If you have the Volume I and Volume II books, you are already skilled in seeing the different layers. But, if not...the black lines in these seam designs are stitched first (these are the Base Seams). Then, add any other thread embroidery (except any that are accents on top of silk ribbon stitches in the designs). Next add the silk ribbon embroidery stitches. Last, add any sequins or beads to the seam. If you are unsure of what an "object or stitch is" look at the SYMBOL KEY on Pages 120-121 for help.

If you need help with creating a specific stitch or silk ribbon embellishment; check out the tutorials on shawkl.com blog and read the next section on Embroidery Stitches.

Each seam in this book includes different ideas

and a variety of silk ribbon flowers or thread embroidery stitches. However, all of these are simple to create.

Each also follows the same sequence for creation: Mark the crazy quilt block using the template (or free-hand stitch and don't use the templates); embroider the Base Seam; add other embroidery stitches; add silk ribbon stitches; add beads, buttons, sequins, etc.

SHAPE TEMPLATES -- These are usually based on common geometric shapes (squares, circles, polygons, etc.) and multiple peaks/valleys (like rolling curves) as tracing guides for marking.

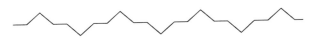

Usage Instructions --
Step 1:
Prepare the shape template according to the "Create Templates instructions". Align the edge with the design along the seam. Just as with the Stitch Templates, you can choose to align over the seam line, or slightly above/below the line depending on how you want the embroidery to flow across the seam.

Step 2:
Using your marking tool, draw a line along the edge of the template shape.

Step 3:
Select an embroidery stitch to create along the drawn line. It can be any stitch that will allow you to follow the line. My favorites are Stem Stitch, Back Stitch, Wrapped Back Stitch, Outline Stitch, and Blanket Stitch. You can however use any stitch that will allow you to follow along this drawn line.

Use the stab method (rather than the scoop method) to embroidery the chosen stitch along the seam if you are hooping your work. Once stitched, this completes the Base Stitch. Next, you can add other embroidery (thread and ribbon) to expand this seam into any of the designs in this book. The steps are the same as for the Stitch Templates section.

Remember to simply layer your silk ribbon embroidery, beads, sequins, etc. on top of the base stitch just created.

Sequence of layers:

Base Seam and other Embroidery -

Next add any Silk Ribbon Embroidery -

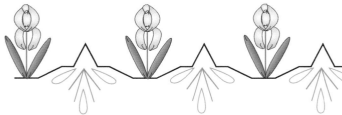

Last, add beads/sequins/etc.

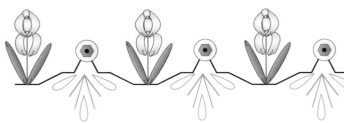

OBJECT TEMPLATES -- Further embroidery of the basic seam, after using either the SHAPE or STITCH templates, can include a variety of simple embroidered objects or lines.

Some of these can also be templated to ensure a uniform spacing and size across the seam. A 3-9 prong fan shape, a specific grouping of silk ribbon stitches, or even a butterfly shape can be easily created after first using a template to mark the needle placement positions. Therefore, the last template of this book is a variety of the extra thread or ribbon embroidery elements used in the seam designs within the book...and some extras to get you thinking of new seams! I love working with templates! They are a bit of work to create, but for a couple of hours of effort I save countless hours in frustration.

Embroidery Stitches:

The thread embroidery stitches in these seam designs are quite basic. They include: Back Stitch, Wrapped Back Stitch, Chevron Stitch, Creten Stitch, Feather Stitch, French Knot, Herringbone Stitch, Outline Stitch, Stem Stitch and Straight Stitch. Instructions for these are easily located on the web or in general Embroidery Books. Most of them are also covered in the CRAZY QUILTING VOLUME I: BEYOND THE BASICS (pages 99-101).

The silk ribbon embroidery stitches are also very basic but do require some practice if you are a true novice. The seams in this book include these ribbon stitches: Straight Stitch, Stab Stitch (Japanese Ribbon Stitch), Woven Stitch, French Knot, Stem Stitch, and Detached Chain Stitch. Instructions on how to create these stitches and the specific flowers included in these seam designs (created with these stitches) are included in the CRAZY QUILTING VOLUME II: RIBBON EMBELLISHMENTS book (pages 50-69).

Symbol Key

The seam designs are built with basic embroidery stitches, beads/sequins, and silk ribbon flowers. While these are easy to understand by the diagrams, here is a sampling of the most common items and their corresponding name.

It is also important to understand that any object in these designs can be substituted with another shape of the same item, or even with a different item. For instance, a sequin can be omitted and replaced with a small button.

Any item of the same size can also be swapped, even if the objects are not of the same type. For instance, if the diagram shows a silk ribbon rose, you can change that to a clay rose bead or even to a sequin is you prefer.

So, mix up these designs to fit the objects in your own stash.

SEQUINS

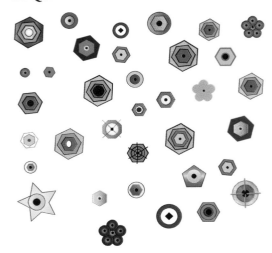

Sequins come in a huge variety of shapes, sizes, and color. They may be metal or plastic types. You can mix the sizes and shapes by stacking them or use as an individual element. I prefer the 3mm to 8mm sizes for stacking.

These seam designs include round, polygon, star, and flower shaped. Primarily these are mostly flat. However, there are cupped sequins that work beautifully, they just are more difficult to draw.

Secure by placing a bead over the center hole (one that is larger than the hole) and sew up through the sequin(s) through the bead and back down through the sequin(s) again. Repeat at least once more. If you like, you can also create Straight Stitches from the outside edge of a sequin to the center, and repeat enough times to hold it in place.

Thread ~ Floss ~ Cording

Detached Chain Stitches

You can easily use 6-strand floss or perle cotton for embroidery of the Base Seam and the additional embellishments shown on this page. However, it is even more fun to try metallics, silk cording, yarn, tiny braid and chenille threads for seams!

Detached Chain Stitches with Beads

Straight Stitches

Straight Stitches with Beads

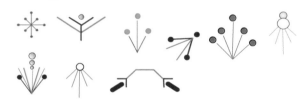

Round Beads can be easily substituted with other shapes, sizes, colors. Crystals and Montees are also good choices.

Straight Stitches & Detached Chain Stitches

Straight Stitches & Detached Chain Stitches with Beads or French Knots

Optional: Bullion Knots

117

SILK RIBBON

Stab Stitch (Japanese Ribbon Stitch)

Detached Chain Stitch

Detached Chain Stitch & Stab Stitch

Use 2mm or 4mm (usually) for ribbon work done on seams because the scale is so small.

Work to manipulate the ribbon so that it does not twist (unless that is the specific look you are wanting).

Group Detached Chain Stitches, Straight Stitches and Stab Stitches to create butterflys, flowers and fans.

Watch the direction of the Detached Chains in the Seam Designs as some begin at the base of a bud while others begin at the tip.

Straight Stitch

French Knot (or beads)

Loop Stitch

Fly Stitch Rose
(Melanies Rose)

Woven Rose

Fargo Rose

Wrapped Back Stitch (or Bullion Thread Stitch, or Rice Beads)

BEADS

Round Beads and Seed Beads

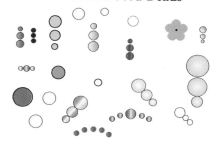

Beads come in a variety of color, shape, luster and size. These seam designs mostly include round beads, but you can substitute with any bead you like.

My preference for seams is: 2mm to 4mm size round beads; 3mm to 4mm rice beads, 3mm to 4mm bugle beads, 3mm crystal bicones or crystal rounds, size 11 uniform shaped seed beads (round and square) and 15mm rocailles.

Beads and Thread Embroidery

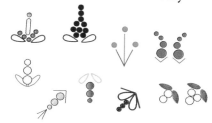

Also, you can find jewelry and clothing adornment items that sew on. One of these is the "montee" which is not truly a bead, but acts like a bead. It is a stone set in a jewelry prong setting, with channels at the back for sewing. I have added a few of these to the Seam Designs, but you can easily substitute with any 3mm or 4mm bead in your bead stash.

Bugle Beads and Rice Beads

Montee'

Techniques on Surface Area Beading are included in the CRAZY QUILTING VOLUME I: BEYONDTHE BASICS *book (pages 128 - 139).*

BUTTONS

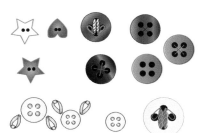

Secure buttons with thread. Then, add tiny beads to cover this thead; or use decorative thread to cover. Tiny Bullion flowers can be created with Detached Chain leaves to mimic flowers. Turn the button into a flower itself by simply including some leaves in Detached Chain Stitches. The buttons shown are mostly round, but other shapes can also be used.

The templates on the following pages can be scanned into your computer using a scanner/copier and then printed on opaque vellum paper or clear plastic overhead projection sheets. Or, they can be copied directly to the vellum or plastic sheets.

If you prefer the templates to be scaled larger or smaller; you can adjust your printer settings to accomplish this. Printed at 100%, this is the size of templates I prefer using for blocks that measure 12" square and above.

WARNING: Be careful to purchase vellum and/or plastic overhead projection sheets that are made for your type of printer.

If you prefer NOT to copy these directly from your book, you can also go to the author's blog at shawkl.com and dowload a PDF file of these templates. Look at the top of the page for the tab titled: Printable Templates and follow the simple instructions to download and save the file labeled Vol III Fancy Seam Design Templates.

You can also choose to create these seam designs without the use of templates, that is of course perfectly acceptable as well. The templates are only offered to help you and because that is my own preferred method of creating beautiful crazy quilt seams.

Thank you for your book purchase and I hope that you will come to visit me at my blog Shawkl.com sometime.

MY ONLINE SOURCES:

Beads: firemountaingems.com

Ribbon: silkribbon.com, vintagevogue.com and Amazon.com

Threads: Amazon.com, Etsy.com, vintagevogue.com

Sequins: ccartwright.com

Vellum: Amazon.com, the papermillstore.com, jampaper.com

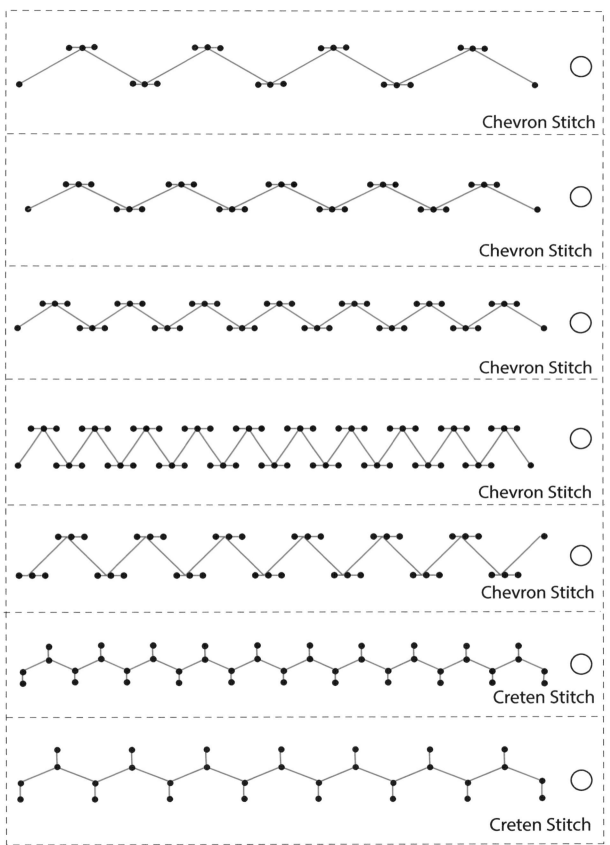

Chevron Stitch ◯

Chevron Stitch ◯

Chevron Stitch ◯

Chevron Stitch ◯

Chevron Stitch ◯

Creten Stitch ◯

Creten Stitch ◯

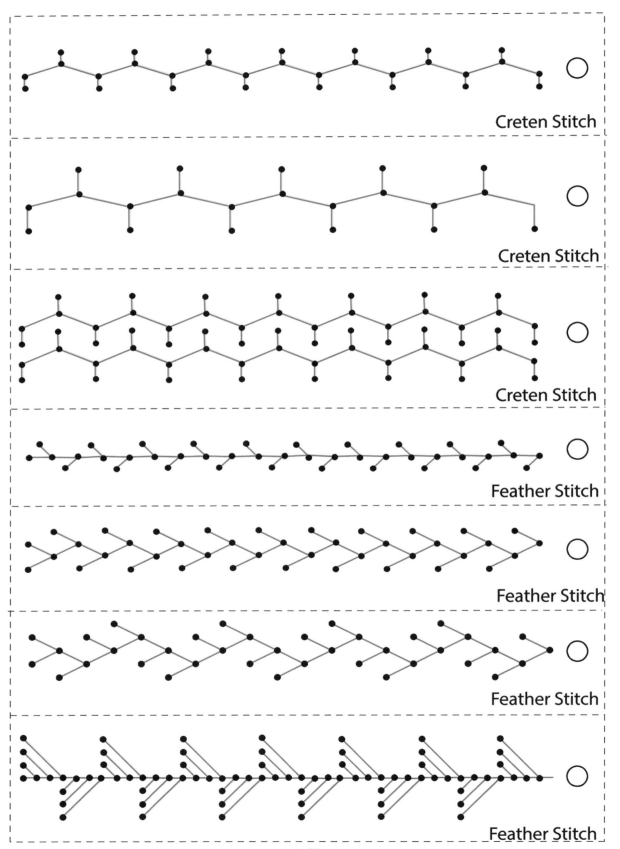

Creten Stitch

Creten Stitch

Creten Stitch

Feather Stitch

Feather Stitch

Feather Stitch

Feather Stitch

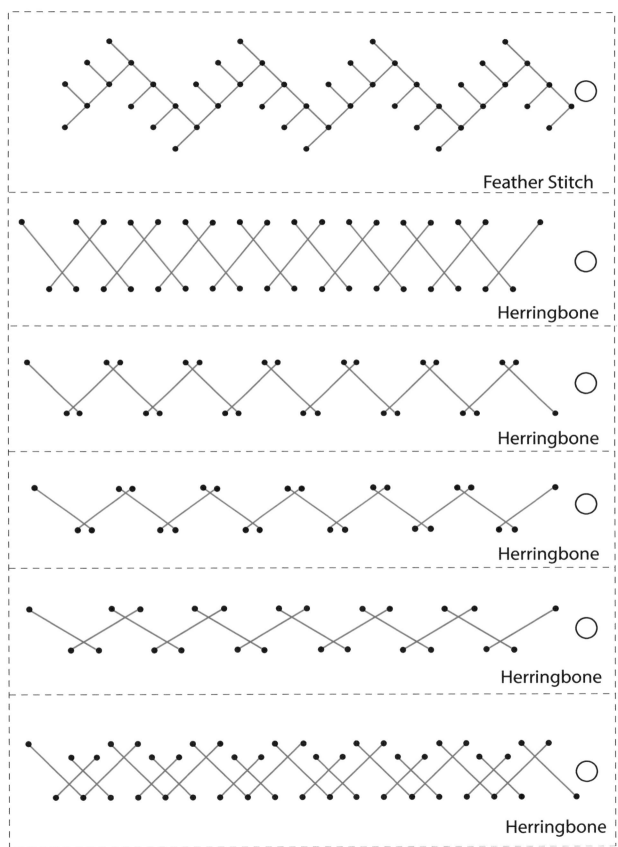

Feather Stitch

Herringbone

Herringbone

Herringbone

Herringbone

Herringbone

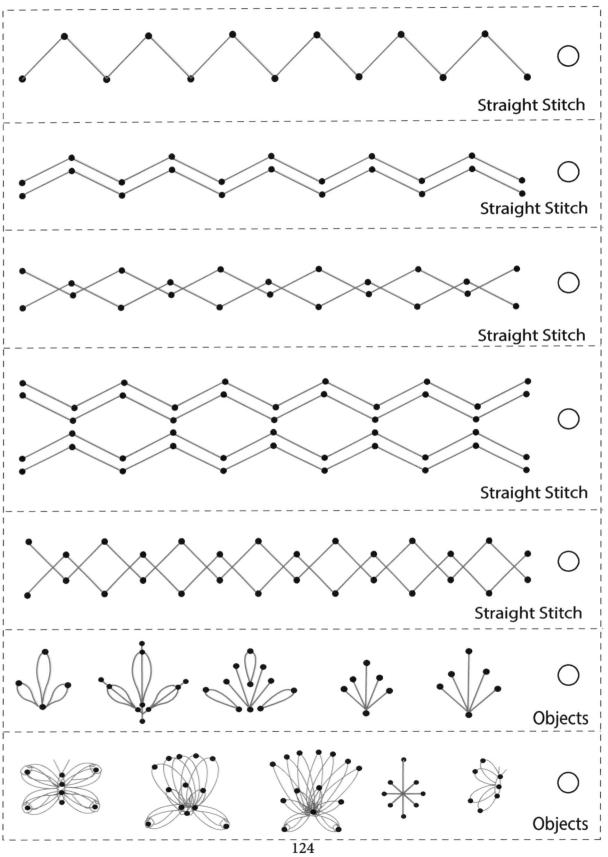

Straight Stitch

Straight Stitch

Straight Stitch

Straight Stitch

Straight Stitch

Objects

Objects

124

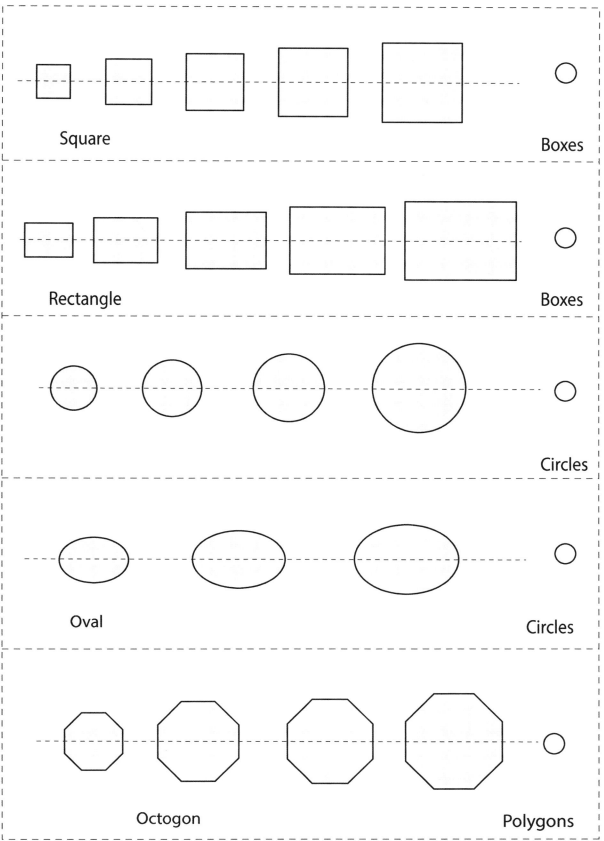

Square   Boxes

Rectangle   Boxes

Circles

Oval   Circles

Octogon   Polygons

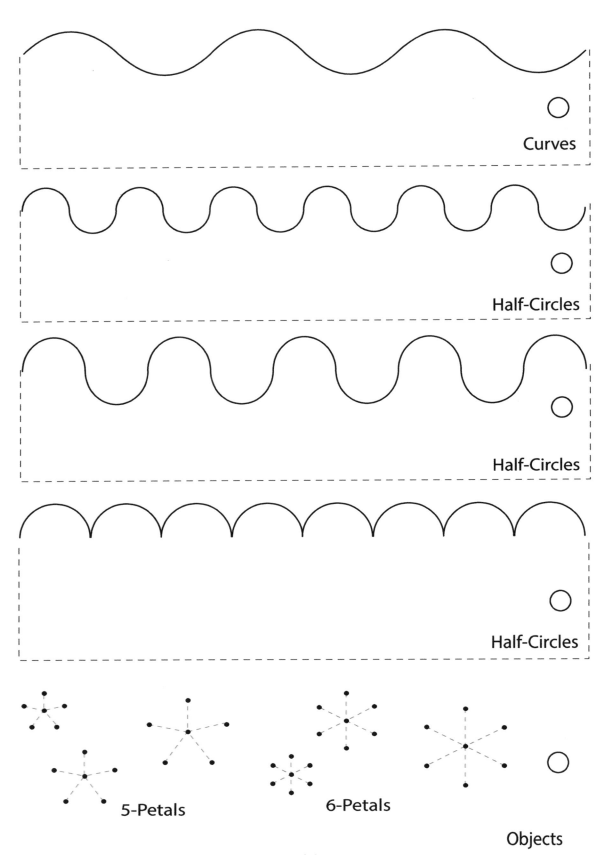

Curves

Half-Circles

Half-Circles

Half-Circles

5-Petals

6-Petals

Objects

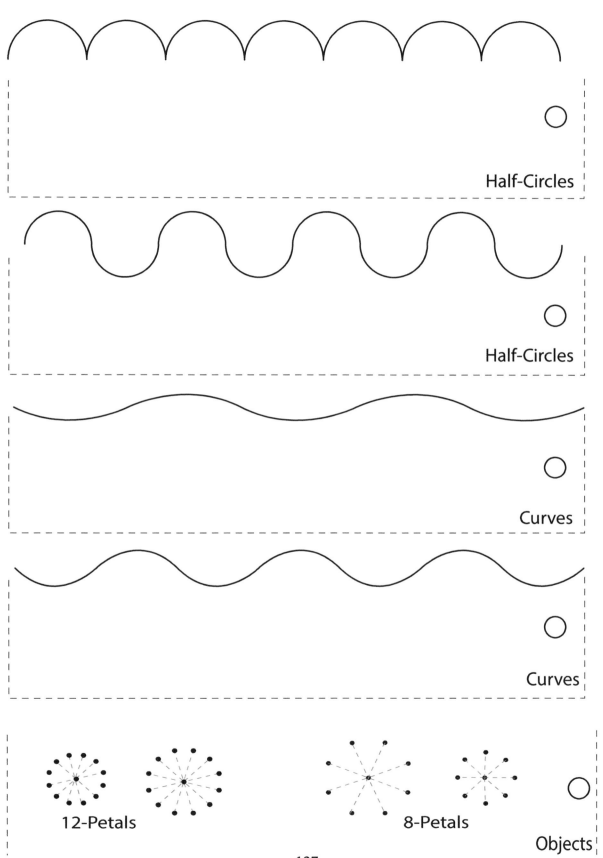

Half-Circles

Half-Circles

Curves

Curves

12-Petals

8-Petals

Objects

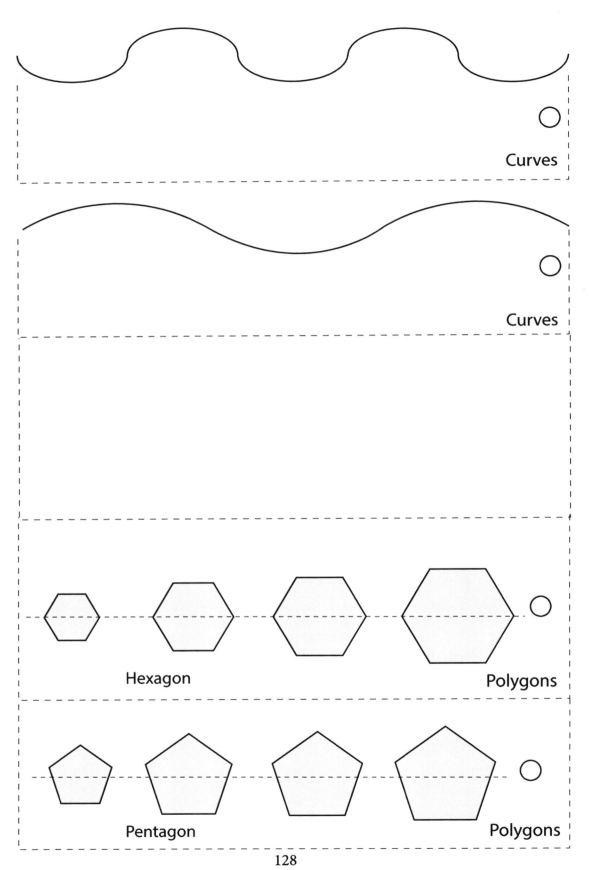

Curves

Curves

Hexagon

Polygons

Pentagon

Polygons

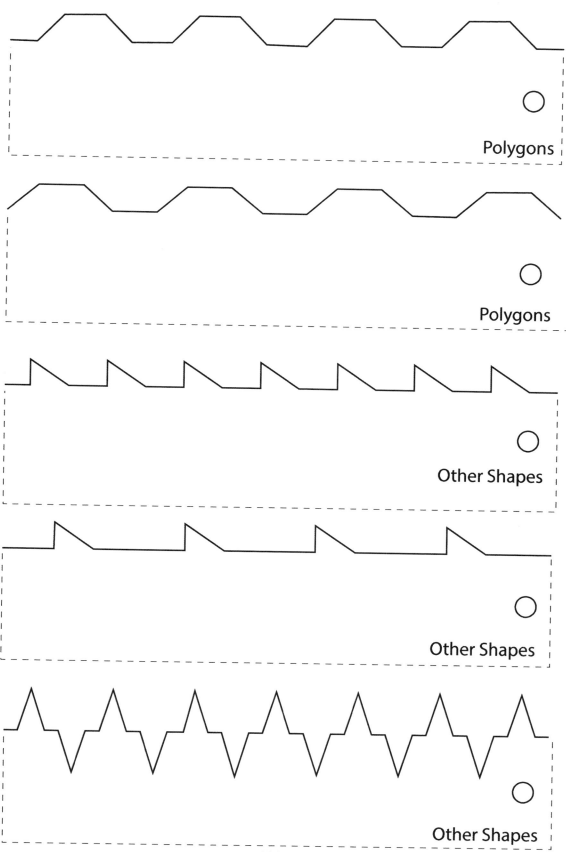

Polygons ○

Polygons ○

Other Shapes ○

Other Shapes ○

Other Shapes ○

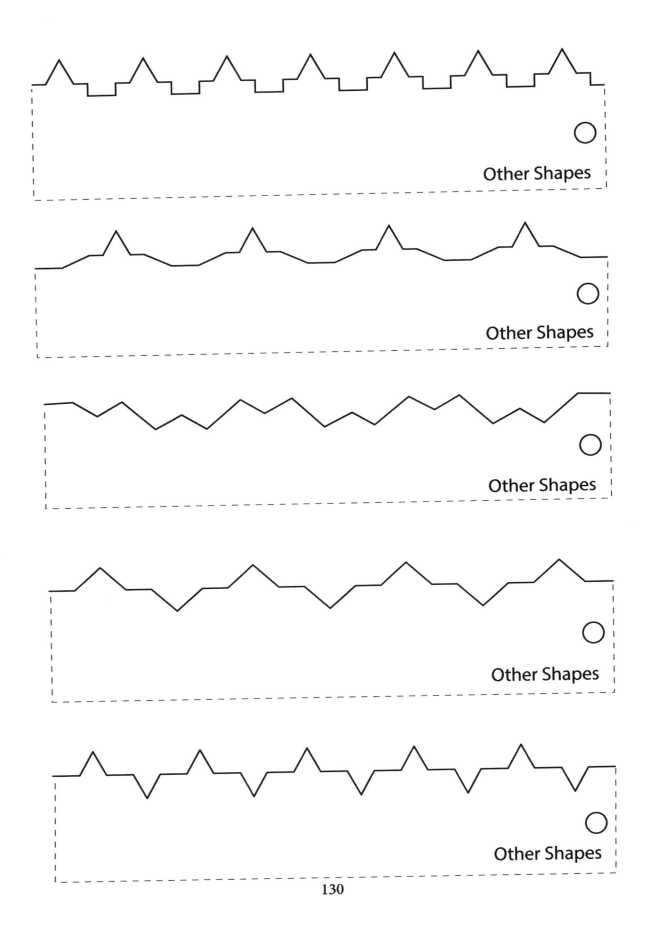

Other Shapes

Other Shapes

Other Shapes

Other Shapes

Other Shapes

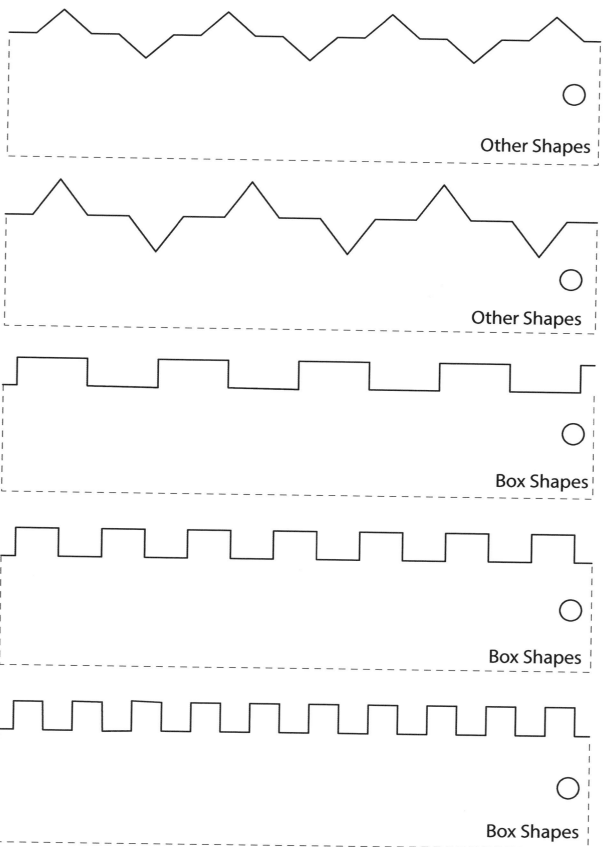

Other Shapes

Other Shapes

Box Shapes

Box Shapes

Box Shapes